RAINHAM
BORN AND BRED

Coral Jeffery

IAN HENRY PUBLICATIONS

ISBN 0 86025 526 3

Dedicated to the memories of

ALICE ELIZABETH COLLIS
and
CHARLES 'WAG' MONTGOMERY

Rainham Born and Bred

Published by
Ian Henry Publications, Ltd.,
20 Park Drive, Romford, Essex RM1 4LH
and printed by
L.P.P.S. Ltd.
128 Northampton Road, Wellingborough
Northamptonshire NN8 3PJ

INTRODUCTION

The Post Office Directory of Essex, 1867, describes Rainham as follows:-

RAINHAM is a village parish, and railway station on the London and Southend Railway, on the Ingerbury brook, in the Southern division of the county, Chafford hundred and rural deanery, Romford union and county court district, Essex archdeaconry, and Rochester diocese, 3 miles north-west from Purfleet steamboat station, 13 from London, 7½ from Grays, 10 from Tilbury, and 5 east from Barking. The village forms a considerable street on the London road, and has a bridge over the Ingerbury brook, and a quay on the creek, at its mouth, in the Thames. The Church of St. Helen and St. Giles is an old structure, with nave, south aisle and porch; the arch separating the nave from the chancel is Norman. The register dates from 1560. The living is a vicarage, annual value £412, with residence, in the gift of John Godsalve Crosse, Esq., and held by the Rev. Henry George Roche, B.C.L. This area is 3,197 acres and the population in 1861 was 987.

Parish Clerk, William Gentry.

John Godsalve Crosse, esq.
Rev. Mortimer Manley, M.A. (Curate) John Plews, esq.

POST OFFICE - Robert Ennever, receiver. Letters arrive at 6 a.m. and 1.30 p.m.; despatched at 2 & 6 p.m. to post office Romford. The nearest money order offices are at Barking & Romford.

NATIONAL SCHOOL - William Jennings, master; Miss Caroline Page, mistress.

CONVEYANCE - Coach to Romford on Wed. only.

RAILWAY TRAINS to London, Tilbury & Southend.

COMMERCIAL

William Blewitt, farmer
Ainger Brooks, wheelwright
James Church, Phoenix public house
John & Thomas Circuit, farmers,
William Clapham, Ferry House
Edward Mee Daldy, coal merchant
Mrs Mary Ennever, shopkeeper
John Farrow, shoemaker
Edward Foard, Angel public house
William Gentry, baker
Isaac Gurnett, market gardener
John Hill, shopkeeper
William Holder, draper

William James Howell, builder
William King, blacksmith
Thomas Wm. Lamber, farmer, South hall
Abraham Manning, farmer, Moor hall
Samuel Mayhew, butcher
Henry Mitchell, farmer
John Wallace Parsons, tailor
Thomas Pease, Bell
Thomas Surridge, farmer
David Tyrrell, shopkeeper
Thomas Willers, saddler
Thomas Wolton, cattle dealer

CHAPTER ONE

THE EARLY YEARS

Rainham, in the County of Essex, lies beside the River Thames 12 miles east of the City of London. This ancient parish, of 3,252 acres, is bounded on the west by the River Ingrebourne, north and north-east by Upminster, and east by Wennington and Aveley, and forms part of the Chafford Hundred.

Man appeared in the area towards the end of the Ice Age, and produced tools from the local flint. Many tools of the Stone Age, dating back 200,00 years have been found during the numerous gravel extractions in the area.

The excavation of a burial ground of the 6th/7th centuries in 1937, between Gerpins Lane and Aveley Road, yielded swords, spearheads, brooches and two green glass drinking vessels. One of the latter, reassembled and now in the British Museum, gives its name to the Saxon Horn public house nearby. The name Rainham came from the Saxons. In the British Museum a Charter of A.D. 697 states that Hodilred, a Saxon dignitary, grants land to Ricingahaam (Roegingaham). The name has been transmuted through Renham, Reynham and Raynham into Rainham, which, according to some, could mean 'settlement of the ruling people'. Other historians hold the view that it comes from Ryne, meaning stream or watercourse, and Ham - hamlet or village.

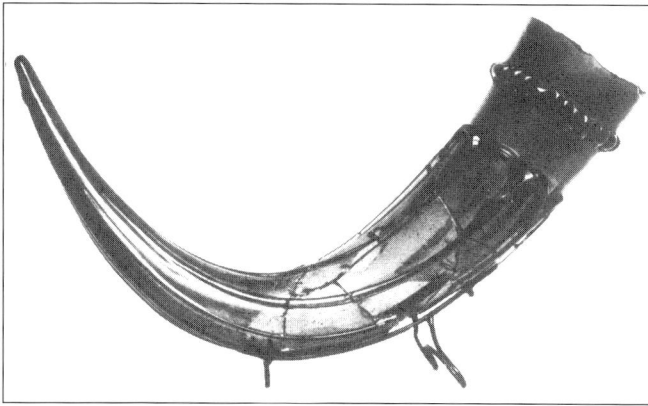

Several finds from the Roman occupation of around A.D. 150, were discovered at various locations in Rainham. In 1928 workmen unearthed a stone coffin to the north of New Road. The coffin contained two bodies, one apparently female, a glass cup and a small gold coin of Tetrachus A.D.267-273. The coffin and its contents were removed to Colchester Castle Museum. Wally, an old gentleman who resided in Cherry Tree Lane, had lived at Mardyke Farm at this time. When I was young I would sometime 'run errands' for him. He would say, "fetch us in a paper, and I'll show you the teeth of them dead 'uns." He said he had removed a couple of the gold teeth from the coffin, but whether the pieces of metal he proudly showed to all and sundry, were actually the teeth we'll never know.

Numerous finds of the first and second centuries A.D. were unearthed from the foundations of the Mardyke Estate. This resulted in one of the tower blocks being named Roman House.

In 1066 Rainham had a population of 190. Twenty years later this had increased to 220, living in 43 households. Rainham wasn't to expand for several centuries. In the 17th century only 44 households are recorded.

Bridge Road leads from the A1306 at Dover's Corner to Rainham Broadway. Due to repeated flooding from the River Ingrebourne over the past centuries, the terraced cottages there were known locally as Flood Row.

Rainham bridge was first mentioned in 1234 and in 1356 it was a broken plank bridge, when Thomas de Hoggeshawe undertook to repair it.- partly at his own cost and partly with voluntary contributions; the King, who often used the bridge when hunting, granted Hoggeshawe protection for his men, carts and materials, for two years.

In 1623 the bridge was broken again, and its repair was said to be the duty of the lords of Berwick and South Hall manors, in Rainham. In 1641 it was a stone bridge. In 1774 it became known as Red Bridge, and in 1834 it was described as a wooden bridge, and its repair was shared by the marsh bailiff and the lord of Berwick. It was taken over by Essex County Council in 1892, and rebuilt in 1898.

Apart from our Georgian buildings, the structure of the village is, in the main, late Victorian/early Edwardian as this was when the population of Rainham began to expand.

The church stands in the centre of the Village, a fine Norman structure built around 1170 by Richard de Lucy, a son-in-law of Henry II. It is the oldest church within the Borough of Havering, and the only church in the country dedicated to St Helen & St Giles.

Until recent years a handsome clock with brass pendulum and weights and housed in an oak case stood in the Church tower. It bore the inscription:- "The cost of this clock for the vestry was raised in two days by Edward Leonard Button, aged 12, and Arthur Edward Kelley, aged 9. All Saints Day, 1892". Both lads were choir boys, Edward being the younger son of the harness maker, later pictured outside the smithy in Upminster Road South. He is the tall youth wearing an overcoat, and was a clerical worker at Frog Island Cement Works. He later emigrated. Arthur Kelley sadly passed away aged 15½ years and lies beside his father in Rainham Churchyard

Next to the churchyard stands Rainham Hall, now in the ownership of the National Trust. It was built in 1729 in the Dutch Style by Captain John Harle, owner of Rainham Wharf. The square plan and equal elevation is reminiscent of houses on Dutch paintings, the varied colour of the bricks giving pattern to the walls. The ornamental cornice beneath the roof and the stone quoins over the rounded windows are to be seen from the front elevation. The railings and gate are of the best work of the time and the finely carved wood of the Corinthian front porch is remarkable. The interior is spacious with black and white marble floors to the entrance hall, a decorative archway opens on to a fine staircase and the doorway into the dining room is elaborately carved. All the rooms are wood panelled. There are large gardens and decorative urns, one in the former Dutch garden is ten feet high.

The smaller house beside the Hall is The Lodge. In 1945/6 the Red Cross started a branch there (called Essex 222) when it was the home of Mrs. Hussey, Headmistress of Rainham Primary School.

The wedding of Grace Fitch to Cyril Spinks, 1898. Grace was a servant at Rainham Hall

The Redberry, a tall red brick house, stands next to The Angel. The frontage is late 18th century, though brickwork at the rear suggests an earlier date. Before her marriage to Mr Swann, Miss C Earps kept two horse drawn coal wagons at the rear of the Redberry. From the 1930's until 1958, Miss M Swann ran a small private school here for children aged 5 to 8: I attended this school in 1952. Every so often during lessons Miss Swann would turn her back to the class and lift the front of her skirt. We, the pupils, would crane our tiny necks to see what she was doing and she, with a flourish, would produce a handkerchief from the leg of her navy bloomers.

Elizabeth Gunning Fitch, Grace's younger sister, seated 2nd row on the left, was photographed in 1899 when 'in service' aged 16 years. It was common practice for sisters to work for the same household, often following in the footsteps of their mother and grandmother

The house next to The Redberry was purchased by former Vicar, Samuel Kekewich, to serve as a Vicarage. In 1710 William Finch of Berwick Manor, Patron of the church, rebuilt it at his own expense.

The old Phoenix was totally destroyed by fire in 1891 and, like its namesake, rose from the ashes in its present form. The design is such that it complements Rainham Hall, which stands directly opposite.

Mayhew's butcher's shop and the Phoenix.
The small building beyond the inn was Broadbent's Estate Agents

The new Angel Inn was rebuilt in 1907 in the same style as its predecessor.
Until the early 1960/70s the interior remained unchanged with small seating areas
within glass and wood partitions.
My grand-dad said they reminded him of Confessionals

The Bell was reconstructed in Mock Tudor style. The projecting upper chamber, supported by posts and wall on the footway, provides an interesting entrance to the village. It was reputedly constructed to give the invalid wife of the landlord an outlook over the village.

My mother, Alice Hockley, born 1908, recalls the village of her childhood;- "The Green stood in the centre of the Village. Grandfather remembered a duck pond there, but that was a bit before my time. Over the years the green had reduced in size, but was still the focal point of the Village. On warm summer evenings Uncle Russell would play the fiddle while his daughter Lily, danced to his lively tunes, encouraged and applauded by patrons of the Bell and Angel, who soon joined in, and the sound of enjoyment filled the air. They were happy times.

The Village centre consisted of the Church, Rainham Hall and the Redberry. There was a cook shop where you could buy hot saveloys, faggots and peas pudding, a General Store, Stationers, Dairy, Bank and Post Office. Parsons the Tailors was across from the Green and Mr Parsons would sit, cross-legged, in the window sewing.

Swann's Wharf was behind the Redberry. The slaughterhouse, Mayhews, was next to Charlotte's Alley where there were some old wooden cottages and a pump. Schoolboys would peep through the gaps in the weatherboard to watch the poor animals being poleaxed.

My Aunt Grace was in service at Rainham Hall. She would scare us with tales of the smugglers' ghosts who lurked in the tunnels which she said ran from the Hall to the Phoenix, then on to the Thames.

The River Ingrebourne, which became Rainham Creek at Red Bridge, often flooded the cottages in Bridge Road - which became known locally as Flood Row. The tenants would move all their belongings, including livestock, upstairs with them until the waters subsided."

THE WAR MEMORIAL

The picture is of the unveiling ceremony for Rainham's Memorial to the Fallen of the Great War. Around 1919 William 'Punch' Montgomery began a collection for a permanent memorial to honour his friends who never came back, as he did, from the Great War, and raised the princely sum of £60. The contractor chosen to build the memorial was Mr Lucey, who had difficulty working to the specifications, as the architect had designed it with brick niches for statues or vases. Local builder, William 'Doodles' Vinton was advised 'not to get involved' as this would be too difficult to build as niches were usually constructed in concrete. Not to be outdone, he studied the plans and completed the brickwork himself, giving his services free of charge.

On the advice of Baker, Hammond and Laver, the memorial was of Belgian bricks, brought by barge to the village by the Thames and Rainham Creek to Town Wharf.

After completion the bricks, being so soft, should have been 'rubbed over', but one of the contractors 'tuck pointed' them with a trowel, which was to cause deterioration some thirty years after.

UNVEILING OF RAINHAM WAR MEMORIAL,

Sunday, November 7th, 1920, at 3.30 p.m.

Order of Service

Before long the memorial became known as 'the clock tower'. In 1924, incensed by this lack of respect, Mr Montgomery successfully took action against the bus company for showing this as the destination, the Court finding in his favour and ordering the company to change tickets and destination boards to show Rainham War Memorial.

On 25th March, 2002, at the request of the Rainham Preservation and Improvement Society, the War Memorial was Listed as Grade II.

Keep's Shoot and Jetty, Rainham Ferry, 1892

A barge on Rainham Creek

CHAPTER TWO

A WALK THROUGH THE VILLAGE

Rainham was a very tight knit community, and some of the old characters who ran the shops around the turn of the century are remembered here by Ruth, who was born in Rainham in 1914;- "The shop next to the Bell was Kingsbury's the grocers. This shop passed hands several times - to Mr Desmond, who sold to Palmer's, who sold on to Green's Stores. Later branches opened in Wennington and Upminster Roads.

"Fred Blow's bakery came next. He later sold this business to Beard's who traded there for many years before selling on to Barton's the Bakers as a going concern.

"There was an alleyway between this and the next shop where Artie Cook sold greengrocery and wet fish; he also sold fried fish and chips, cooked in an outhouse behind his shop. Eve remembers her mother, in the late 1920s, buying two tuppenny pieces of fish and three penn'orth of chips for the family tea each Friday. They would round the meal off with 4 jam puffs purchased from Beard's for threepence. Total cost of the meal, tenpence.

"Next came the newsagents owned by Fred Harris which later passed on to Elvey's. A sweetshop and tobacconist called The Bijou (pronounced By-jo by locals) was owned by Mr & Mrs Arnold Clarke. The business was later sold to Mr Sanders, whose daughter married the son of Mr Perthen, the jeweller.

"Mr Holmes transferred his Post Office and stationers here in 1911. This became Barclay's Bank a few years on. Mr Joslin's Tea Rooms came next and was known locally as The Cook Shop. He sold to Rushton's, who sold to Oakley's, who sold on to Smithers, who lived here with his two sons. Mr Smithers was a strange character; it was alleged that he gave sanctuary to Frederick Browne and William Kennedy, the two hanged for the murder of P.C. George Gutteridge of Stapleford Abbotts in 1927. He regularly appeared in Court and was

described as a 'thoroughly bad lot' when at Grays Court he threw his hat at Judge Crawford. Once after a spell 'away' he returned with a blood soaked handkerchief around his neck! He would write slogans on the windows of his shop stating 'fresh murders done daily' - local children were terrified of him.

"Next came two cottages. Lou Parker, shoemender, lived here. He sold out to J G Beard of Hornchurch, the first dairyman in Rainham. This later became Durley's Dairy. Mrs Sears was housekeeper for Durley's in the 1920s, and worked two mornings per week for 4 shillings (20p). Ray was a milkboy for Durley's when he left school in 1944, until he was conscripted into National Service. He would deliver milk, by cycle, to Salamon's Factory in Ferry Lane. He progressed to a handcart and later to a horse and cart. When his horse, Dolly, died Ray had to collect another horse from Grays and walk it back to Rainham.

Durley's dairy, 1930s

"L M Goodwin traded at this shop for many years, which remained a Gent's Hairdressers until the death of his descendent, Ivan, in the late 1980's. Eve remembers Ivan's sister, Gwen, providing a ladies' hairdressing service at the premises during the 1920/30's, her speciality being the 'bingle' - her own adaptation of the 'bob' and the 'shingle'. In 1995 the shop was purchased by Rainham Church and is now the much-loved Ship Centre.

"The next shop was occupied by Mr Frank Phillips Hill, then Mr Harry Holmes, seller of boots and shoes, lived here before the Great War. While he was in the forces the business was sold on to Mr Lampard who had a coal round, and stabled his horses behind the shop. This later became Cutbush the Florists.

"A yard owned by Charlie Bridge, Haulage Contractor, was on this site. Alf Burr, shoemender, originally had half of this shop, which he shared with Mr & Mrs Ennever (on left). Burrs eventually took over the complete shop, where they sold shoes for many years.

"Jim Brown the barber lived here with his wife and two children, Charlie and Dorothy. This shop is now Kenton's Hairshop.

Mr Hill is pictured outside his first shop in the Village.

Mr Hill and his assistant, Keith

"F P Hill, purveyor of Fruit & Veg., Fish & Rabbits, came next. Haddock, kippers and bloaters were smoked in oak dust in a smokehole behind the shop. Each Friday they would sell hot fish and chips, fried in a small outhouse. Elsie would call the orders from a rear window

and, when ready, Carrie would walk through the alley and along the road to the shop, carrying a tray of steaming fish and chips on her head.

"Mr Lonnon (on the left), a German, ran a chemist shop here. He was quite a character. One day a young lady asked for 'Amami' shampoo (a new product), to which he replied, "Blow Amami, this is the one I sell, you'll have that." Another customer asked for Beechams Pills, he said, "I must charge you one and threepence, but they're only worth fourpence halfpenny, box included. They're nothing but Hudson's Powder and soft soap." Mr Lonnon also extracted teeth, using ether, at this rather dingy establishment.

"Farrow's had a drapery and boot and shoe shop here. They sold out to Self's who were drapers and haberdashers. Next came the sweet shop owned by Miss Sutcliffe, who sold out to Mr & Mrs Fred Rush. Mrs Bridge sold groceries here, assisted by Jessie Hockley (pictured with her young sister Alice in 1913), who took up nursing in the 1920s and later became Matron of St George's Hospital, Hornchurch. Mr Payne took over this shop after the death of Mrs Bridge.

"Mr Warwick traded as a builders' merchant in this shop which later became Dennis's Tool Shop. Mr Maskell sold groceries and drapery here, until the business passed on to Mr Buss. Roe's later had the general store here which was eventually taken over by Flint's. Next came the cottages known as Pit Place. Mr Perthen had a jewellery shop here.

"There was an ex-servicemen's hut between Perthens and the cottages, which was used for shows and musicals. .

"On the opposite side of Upminster Road, known as Back Street at this time, were Mr Hill's mother and sister, Nellie (pictured on the far right in 1931), in a toy shop, next to the churchyard. From the 1950's it became first Freda's, then Annette's, ladies' hairdressers. In the 1980s it was a record shop called "Disco 2 + 2".

"The Post Office originally stood here. In the early 1900s Hartley Jennings was postmaster and Mrs Holmes, clerk. When the annual visits were made to the Post Office from head office, Mr Jennings would ask his assistant to take a cheque to Barclays to change for cash. He would then put the money into the till. When the 'officer's' visit was over, he would then take the cash back to Barclays who would, in turn, return his cheque. In 1907 there was a 'mysterious' fire, which resulted in the departure of Mr Jennings and Mrs Holmes being appointed postmistress. The Post Office later moved across the road and Payne's transferred their business here, where they traded as butchers for many years.

The Broadway: in centre Mr Holmes's Post Office

"Next came the cottage where the Nichols family lived. Ben and Eliza Hockley lived in the next cottage with their five children, Harry, Ben (my Grand-dad), Alice, Harriet and Hannah. Harriet later married William 'Punch' Montgomery, first president of Rainham Working Men's Club. Miss Cook later had a ladies' fashion shop here and in 1973 Oxfam opened a Charity

13

Shop. These shops now form the Goldmine 'complex'. Sturgess butcher's shop on this site later became Arnold's.

"Reed's had a saddlers here. This later became Cramphorn's Corn & Seed Merchants. When I was small my Gran would send me here to buy a pound of hoof and horn and grit for her chickens. The chickens ate grit to harden the eggshells. Next there was a thatched bungalow owned by Mrs Blows, who often had eggs for sale. This lovely dwelling was demolished to make way for St Helen's Court.

"On the far side of Broadway and next to the Vicarage, Mr Parsons had a tailor's shop. Mr Jaggs was his assistant.

"Dave Saitch lived in the cottage next door. He wasn't a trained vet but he was very good with animals, particularly horses. Next came Charlotte's Alley (right) with its wooden houses and pump. Mayhew's butcher's shop and abattoir came next, with its unusual slate pentroof on wooden posts projecting over the footpath. This building, originally cottages, was over 200 years old when demolished in 1964 to make way for the Stanton Radio building, now the Branch Library.

Slaughterhouse staff around 1900

"The Swedish Timber Company woodyard, known as Station Wharf, was to the right of The Angel and on the bank of Rainham Creek. In 1927 it was acquired by John Newman Ltd., who traded there until the 1970s. Rainham Creek was navigable until the 1960s with motor tank boats taking over from the barges that had been a familiar sight at this spot until 1938. The site is now a pleasant open space funded by Cleanaway Havering Riverside Trust.

Lynne, born in 1946, tells us a little of Salamon & Company:

"My father, Clifford Bond, was born in 1910 in old Dagenham village. My mother was born in Chequers Lane Cottages (known as Coaley Row), Dagenham Dock, in 1908, the year the railway station was opened. Cottages with bay windows were known as Piano Row, being thought to be a bit better class!

"They married in 1939 and bought a new house in Rainham. Dad worked as a driver and motor fitter on sand and ballast lorries in the area. He then worked for Wag Bennett & Sons for a number of years, then finally in Ferry Lane for Salamon & Company.

"Salamons was a chemical firm, Mr H E Green being the Director. They produced ether, acids, pitch, tar and other coal products. The had a weighbridge outside their offices, used by the tanker lorries. Their other form of transport was small tanker boats, which used to call at Southend Gas Works, Charlton and Rochester, amongst other places.

"Mr Green told my Dad that he had been one of the first to bring sailing barges into Rainham Creek. There was an old photo of a barge in the Creek with a large 'S' on the sails – perhaps this was one of his barges. Names of some of the later motor boats were *Tartartic, Saltar, Ether, Margery Jean* and *Brenda* – the latter two being from Mr Green's family.

"The tankers used to moor in Rainham Creek or, depending on the tide, at Murex jetty. As a child I liked nothing better than being invited on to the boats via the deep jetty steps. I remember Dad taking me and lots of friends to see the Royal Yacht *Britannia* go downstream.

"Salamons was taken over by North Thames Gas and finally shut down in 1969."

Clifford Bond on *Saltar* (Salamon's tar) in Rainham Creek

CHAPTER THREE

THE EXPANSION OF RAINHAM

THE RAILWAY
In 1854 the London, Tilbury, Southend railway line was opened as far as Tilbury with the station at Rainham linked by ferry to Gravesend, Kent. The first train passed through Rainham on 10th April, 1854. The line was extended to Southend in 1856. The weatherboard station was built after a fire in 1891 and was replaced by the current station in 1961.

THE FIRE BRIGADE.
A volunteer fire brigade of 12 men was formed in 1904 and a fire station built at the corner of Parkway and Upminster Road South in 1914. In 1933 the brigade replaced its handcart with a motor-driven fire engine. Hornchurch brigade took over from Rainham in 1936. A new fire station was built at Wennington in 1962 at a cost of £35,000.

In the monthly report book kept by Capt. Lazell from 1929 to 1934 states:- "At 6.30 one evening the telephone bells rang summoning the men to man the engine to White Post Corner. No fire was traced. When they returned to the Station they saw that a kite on the wire had set the bells off."

RAINHAM CLINIC.
The Clinic, established by Romford Rural District Council was opened 1st June, 1921. Those present included Cllr. Mrs Parchment, Dr. A Ball and health visitor Nurse Fawcett. A committee was formed, consisting of Mrs Ayres, Mrs Hearn, Mrs Mace (wife of Headmaster of Rainham Primary School), Mrs Bennett and Mrs Hadencu. Eight mothers attended and there seemed to be every prospect that the clinic would be greatly appreciated.

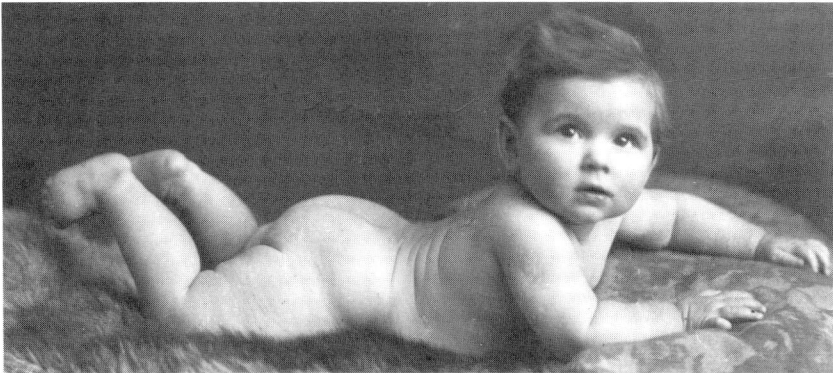

My sister Iris was one of the babies to benefit from the new clinic.

THE SCHOOLS
Rainham School, designed by East Ham architect John Dennison, built in 1872, is the oldest school building within the Borough of Havering still used for educational purposes. The

expansion of Rainham during the last century resulted in the addition of a new hall and classrooms in 1933; a secondary school in Lambs Lane (Chafford) in 1950; La Salette Roman

Rainham Village School, 1912

Catholic Primary School, Dover's Corner in 1957; Parsonage Farm School, Allen Road, in 1965; and Brady School, Wennington Road, in 1969. South Hornchurch Board School, in Blacksmiths Lane came into existence in 1899. When it was enlarged in 1912, Mr W Softly of Ford Lodge gave a 'treat' and party for the children in celebration.

Rainham Village School, 1920/21.

Fancy dress at Rainham School, 1935

Rainham School football team with Mr Mace & Mr Daniels,1937/8

Rainham Junior School 1952

Carol concert 1955

Rainham Secondary School 1959/60

CHAPTER FOUR

PLACES OF WORSHIP

ST HELEN AND ST GILES

St Helen (247-327) is reputedly British and, by her marriage to an upper-class Roman officer serving in this country, became the mother of Constantine the Great, the first Christian Roman Emperor. She made a pilgrimage to the Holy Land where she discovered the Cross and the sepulchre of the Crucifixion. She is said to have located the nails of the True Cross and had them fashioned into a belt for her warrior son. St Giles was a Greek patrician of the 7th century, who turned to the holy life and was regarded as the patron saint of cripples, beggars and lepers.

Freda, who has worshipped at Rainham Parish Church for many years, tells a little of the church in WWII:- "A barrage balloon broke from its moorings and, as it gradually came down, floated over Rainham dragging its cable, which slewed across the church tower, smashing part of the turret. When the time came to repair it, it was considered too expensive to have it renewed in the original stone, which is why we now have a brick top to the tower.

"After the stained glass had been removed, the windows were boarded up for the duration of the war, so evening services were at 3 o'clock, enabling the congregation to return home before the evening sirens went off. During the blitz people invariably ended up in the vestry, considered to be the safest and strongest part of the church, where they waited for the 'All Clear' before returning home. "There was hardly ever enough coke delivered to keep the boiler going, so in the winter it was extremely cold. Parishioners were encouraged to wrap up warm and bring hot water bottles with them.

"A bomb fell in the far corner of the churchyard, causing graves there to be opened up. For several days curious people came to see the depth of the crater, plus the bones of several bodies, previously interred there. The corner was restored to decorum in a remarkably short time."

THE GOSPEL HALL

The 'iron room' next to the brick building was brought to Rainham from West Thurrock in the mid 1800's, and was demolished in 1984. Prior to this a red corrugated iron building, once used as a Roman Catholic Church, stood on the opposite side of Cowper Road. In about 1938 it was put up for sale, the Catholic Church having been re-located to Dover's Corner.

James Vellacott bought it and let it to the Salvation Army who had started their mission to Rainham in a marquee at the junction of Upminster and Cowper Roads, which was replaced by a wooden building later demolished by a wartime bomb. In the 1930s the wedding of Jessie Hockley and Roy Cottrell at the Gospel Hall is on the right.

The following *Memoirs of the Gospel Hall* is an extract from notes compiled by W G Dalton during 1971, in his 88th year.

"The founder of the work at the Gospel Hall in 1889 was William Spear, a farmer living at East Hall Farm, Wennington, who had come from Tavistock to farm in this area.

The first Mission Hall erected in Cowper Road was the 'iron room' so called as the outer structure was made of corrugated iron. It was soon not large enough to accommodate the congregation attending so Mr Spear had the present Hall erected in 1889. He did not stay at East Hall Farm much longer, and returned to his home county of Devon.

"East Hall thus changed hands and James Vellacott took responsibility for both the Hall and the Gospel Hall. He was about 24 when he came to the farm and his sister, Laura, kept house for him. He later married Miss Morris of Blackheath. Mr Vellacott was a great worker for the hall and its needs, and spent his entire life in the work. The Hall is still known to many as 'Vellacott's Chapel'.

"I attended the Sunday School from the time I was about 8 years old - at that time Mr Spear was Superintendent, this would have been about 1891 and onwards. I can still recall the names of some of the teachers of those early days: J. Baker, Mr Bennett his wife and two daughters, Mr Barnes, Tom Stock, Miss Gregory, John Biggs, just to mention a few. The earliest caretaker I can recall was a Mrs Deacon then Mrs Biggs, Mrs Wood, Mrs Barnard, and now Miss Doris Stebbings.

"Organists over the years that I can recall were Miss Lottie Gregory (who later became Mrs Harry Read), Miss Ethel Cornell, Arthur Cornell, and of more recent years Miss Evelyn Turp, Mrs Frank Wood, and my daughter Ellen.

"The Sunday School excursion in my early days used to be a happy sight as the children (300 or so) marched from the Gospel Hall to the Station to catch 'the Sunday School special' to go to Southend for the day. The numbers of children, parents and friends were so great that a train was hired for these occasions, and even the day school closed for this special day in the year. Sad to say the number of scholars has so decreased in the 1970s that 3 coaches are sufficient for this annual event - to places further afield than Southend."

Eva Montgomery, pictured with her cousin Alice Hockley (seated) at Shoeburyness, whilst on a Gospel Hall 'treat' in 1919. Both wear a ribbon pinned to their dresses to show they are part of a Sunday School outing.

Irene remembers 'the best day of the year':- "When my sister and I were about 6 and 7 years old, we attended Sunday School at the Gospel Hall in Cowper Road. In the school summer holidays Mr Vellacott used to hire a train to take us all to Southend, also a guard's van to take all the prams and pushchairs. We all wore a ribbon pinned to our coats, and marched to the station where our mums were waiting. The village was almost empty. When we arrived at Southend it was off to the beach. After we had a paddle and made our sand pies, we all made our way to the Bee Hive Restaurant on the seafront near the Kursaal, where we were served paste sandwiches, assorted cakes and orange squash. It was bliss! All too soon it was time to catch our train home. At Rainham Station all the dads were waiting for us. You never saw such a tired, happy bunch of children."

The Gospel Hall children are ready to embark on their Sunday School treat in 1957

THE METHODIST CHURCH

The history of Methodism in Rainham goes back to the time of John Wesley, who preached here in 1784, 1785 and 1787, when he made a three day visit to prepare a further edition of the *New Testament*, lodging in Broadway opposite the junction with Ferry Lane. There was a revival and a Hall was built, but the cause died out until a later revival in 1929/30, the original building in Wennington Road was built in 1930.

The following is an extract from the reflections of Bramwell Evans, church steward, on 50 years of the Church, 31st May, 1980:- "Our Church records include a document signed by Rev. Robinson Whittaker and Charles Evans (my father) pledging them both to the bank for £400 advance to purchase the land on which the buildings now stand, and to launch a £4,000 building project. This was at the time of the Great Depression (1928) when their joint income that year scarcely matched the advance. The £4,000 represented approximately ten years joint income at a time when salaries were being annually cut - not raised - to meet inflation. A farm worker's wage was 9 shillings (45p) per week and a doctor's house call cost 5 shillings (25p). Children saw the seaside once a year through their Sunday School outing and the 6 day working week was of 48 hours.

"These folk built a Church and involved themselves in a host of activities witnessing to and caring for a growing community. Then, as now, the ladies spearheaded the fund raising enterprises. I recall many homes where kitchens were dominated by preserving pans with marmalade, chutney, coconut ice, etc., in the making.   Cloth remnants were industriously converted to saleable items at bazaars - social and money raising events.

The Methodist church in 1930

"Men brought personal skills to bear on maintenance, renovation, etc.   Others excavated and built the boiler house and installed central heating, or employed brush and colour in redecorating.

Methodist Youth Club, 1962

"Gifted musicians trained fine choirs for high standard musical events. Dedicated lay people ran the Sunday School and youth work. This was a Church reaching out to the community, and during the war years the building featured as a rest centre for bombed out families, and during weekdays accommodated the local school which was similarly displaced."

Local lad, Wenzel Aylen, often sang at the club. He was a talented singer who toured Britain in the 1960s under the stage name Billy Arnold with 'pop star' Billy Fury. Wenzel died tragically in a fire at his home in Wennington Road when in his thirties.

THE CHURCH OF OUR LADY OF LA SALETTE

The growth of industry, especially the Ford Motor Company, in the Dagenham area in the 1920/30s, led to a rapid increase in population to this area, in particular the Catholic population, due to the arrival of Irish workers.

In 1928, Bishop Doubleday, formerly pastor of Our Lady of la Salette in London, established the mission of St. Peter's as a parish, and confided it to the missionaries of.La Salette. The beginnings of La Salette, Rainham, are tied to the history of St. Peter's. A small mission chapel in Cowper Road was served by the priests of St. Peter's on Sundays. Prior to this, priests from Barking said mass in Rainham.

When the area began to expand the small chapel could not accommodate the increasing congregation. The task of finding a new home for the Catholic Community fell to Fr. John Cotter, a parish priest of St. Peter's. With a borrowed sum of £4,000 the La Salette Fathers purchased land belonging to Dover's Farm. The barn was transformed into a church and the 100 year old farmhouse converted to a presbytery. While a local contractor undertook the job, much of the labour entailed in the conversion was done by men of the parish. The women, not to be outdone, went from house to house collecting such as linen, crockery, etc. Father Cotter was appointed first priest of the new parish by Bishop Doubleday in 1938. The converted church was blessed by him in March, 1939.

During the Second World War Rainham and South Hornchurch were targets for many of Goering's bombers, and a number of parish buildings were destroyed. Fr. Roux, although stationed in Dagenham, was a constant help during these troublesome years. Father William Dolan succeeded Fr. Cotter as parish priest in 1941 and remained here until after the war.

Father Frederick Julien was the third parish priest. He had spent the war years in a Japanese P.o.W. camp in Manila, cheating death by only a few hours when the camp was liberated by the U.S. army. It was Fr. Julien who erected the Sacred Heart War Memorial which graces the parish property. He also built what is known as 'the cottage'.

Fr. Julien's stay in Rainham was brief and he was succeeded by Fr. John Rohrman, who, along with the men of the parish, extended the church facilities and installed a complete sewage system. Fr. Rohrman realised the need for a Catholic school, received permission from Bishop Beck, and began building in 1955. The La Salette Primary School opened in 1957, and is an integral part of the parish. Fr. Rohrman spent 13 years in Rainham and most of the parish property and buildings here are due to his hard work. .He was transferred to Dagenham in 1960.

Fr. Joseph Balgenorth then became parish priest and, under his administration, the school extended. Negotiations were carried out with the Ministry of Transport who purchased some of the property and built a roundabout on the ever busy A13. He also established Sunday evening Mass at La Salette and initiated the weekly bulletin. Although his stay was brief, Fr. Balgenorth made a lasting impression on the parish.

In 1961 Fr. Joseph Nolan succeeded as parish priest. Under his watchful eye many new organisations were brought to life, in the parish. During his 14 years at Rainham a good deal of rebuilding and decorating was accomplished. In 1963 plans were drawn up for a new church and presbytery. In 1965 ground was broken for the new church and more classrooms were added to the school. Fr. Nolan worked to establish a parish social club which was formally opened in 1967. On completion of the new church and presbytery, Bishop Bernard Wall blessed the cornerstone of the church on the 11th October, 1967. La Salette had come a long way from those early days in Cowper Road.

THE BRETHREN

South View Mission Hall in Wennington Road was registered by Brethren in 1902. It became known as Maskell's Chapel, and was supposedly founded by Jeremiah Maskell, a village shopkeeper (1882-1912). It still existed in the 1930s when the members were described as 'Exclusive Brethren', but ceased in the 1950s.

There was also a mission at Smokeholes, Rainham, at the boundary with Upminster.

Coral (sitting second from right) at Ogilvy School of Recovery, Coronation Celebrations, June, 1953

CHAPTER FIVE

THE 'CO-OP'

The Upminster Road branch of the Grays Co-operative Society was opened in 1903, selling grocery, butchery and drapery. The Greenfruit shop adjoining the main building later became the butchery department.

Each member was supplied with a share book and a share or 'dividend' number which was quoted at every transaction within the shop, and also to the milk, bread and coal roundsmen. A dividend was paid twice yearly. For most people now over the age of 40, their Co-op number is engraved on their brain - ours was 12246. My Uncle Sid always told his family to have him buried by the Coop so that they could claim the dividend. They, of course, obliged. After all the Co-op slogan was 'we look after you from the cradle to the grave'.

The Co-op wasn't just a shop, it was a way of life for its members. There was the youth movement, Choirs, drama groups, adult education classes, not to mention the many exhibitions and shows. Handicraft classes for women were held at Rainham Primary School each Friday at 7.30 p.m. Rainham Co-operative Women's Guild was established 3rd September 1935. Meetings were held at Rainham Social Club every Thursday

Guild outing to Clacton on one of Mr. Stephens coaches, 1939.

CHAPTER SIX

THE FERRY

Early industries by the Thames gave rise to a small hamlet of workpeople whose lives centred around the Three Crowns Inn. Mr Bifield recalls his life there during the 1920s and 30s:- "It was 1923 when I first saw Ferry Lane. I was 6 and my parents were contemplating moving to Rainham from Crayford to take over the Three Crowns Inn.

"I don't remember the journey to Rainham via Woolwich pedestrian tunnel but shall never forget getting off the number 23 General Omnibus at Rainham War Memorial, walking past Rainham Hall and wondering who lived in such a large house! It was a Spring Sunday morning and I don't remember seeing any other people. We turned into Ferry Lane from Wennington Road - it was just a mud track to the level crossing with railway workers cottages on the right hand side. Ferry Lane was just a country lane with drainage ditches either side until the Creek bank was reached, then, of course, only one side had a ditch. The only habitation was the Halfway House. The factories of Salamon, Fields and Murex were quiet, no doubt because it was Sunday. I remember climbing up to the river bank and looking at the Thames, then going into the Three Crowns. I don't remember the journey home to Crayford.

"A few months later we moved and I soon became familiar with Ferry Lane. It was one and a quarter miles to Rainham School and the Ferry had children from the Winn, Whitby, Bayford and Ross families, with me and my two sisters making a total of nine. We met at 8 a.m. and it would take just over thirty minutes to school, all would have a packed sandwich lunch.

Rainham School in the 1920s

"So back to Ferry Lane and the mud track to the level crossing. There were three houses on the right, the home of a booking office clerk, the Wright family lived in the centre house, Mr French the station master, whose house was the only one with a front door, the third house accommodated Mr. South the signal box man. Between these houses and the level crossing was the railway goods yard with one siding and a goods shed. On the opposite side of the rail track was a cattle and sheep loading pen. Level crossing gates controlled by the crossing keeper who lived in the cottage opposite the signal box. Past the crossing on the right was a dirt access to Lamson Paragon Sports Ground with just two huts - no pavillion in the early 1920s. Rainham School was allowed to use the ground once a year, we did enjoy that. Opposite the Sports Ground was a field that the Parish Church Choir football team used for home games on a Saturday afternoon, controlled by Mr Cook, the organist and choirmaster. We enjoyed the away games when one of the local bus services - Stephens or Edwards - did the transportation. Above is Rainham's railway station in the 1920s.

"On the left hand side was the main entrance to the Army huts, very often supplemented with many army bell tents, used mostly in the summer for rifle and machine gun practice. A may tree gave name to the bend in the road on the left next to a small brick built sewage pumping station. We could hear the pump working but, as there were no windows, were unable to see anything. Next a sharp right and then left hand bend called 'bendy book', but children called it 'bandy book'. From the Railway to the Halfway House were open fields between the Ingrebourne and Ferry Lane. Halfway House was home to the Hines family and they had a daughter, Florrie, who eventually married Ted May, a Salamon's sailing barge employee, who was nicknamed 'the water rat' as he often swam across the Thames to his home in Dartford. It was he who taught me to swim - in Rainham Creek. Ted later attempted to swim the English Channel, unaccompanied and towing an inflated car inner tube with a fixed bottom containing a bottle of rum and food. He never made it and it was some weeks before his body was recovered. Florrie's grandfather, Mr Starky, made good the potholes in Ferry Lane, which in those days was a very primitive clinker road.

"Salamon's, a chemical works that converted waste products from Gas Works to tar and creosote, had three Thames sailing barges, the *Vendetta, Industry* and *Osborne*, a motorised sailing barge the *Ingrebourne*, a purpose built motor ship *Ether* and, in later years, a new motor ship the *Tartaric* appropriate names for a fleet of tankers with loads between 60 and 120 tons, collecting waste from Gasworks on the Medway and the Thames at Southend. Salamon's also had a road tanker that collected waste from Romford Gasworks.

"Further along Ferry Lane to Cinder Track Corner and the sewage settlement beds, then to the Creek bank and a bend in the road we called Cables' Corner, (an electricity cable from Ferry Lane to T W Ward, under the Creek was installed mid-20's and a sign 'Cable' erected on the riverbank). This lane ran parallel to the Creek bank until the mud track to the Three Crowns, with a left turn to Field's, makers of boot polish, candles and tapers. The candle section closed in the early '20s. Next, two cottages, then Joe Kemp who kept The Little

Wonder sweetshop and tobaconist. He had two older sons George and Fred. Next door, the Bayford family with their schoolgirl daughter, Primrose Daisy May, then the Murex factory main gate and three more cottages, Mr Ross with schoolboy Sid, and in the end house the Whitby family with their school age children.

"Beyond the Three Crowns on the Thames bank a timber house, home of the Winns, also with schoolchildren. Two other homes at Rainham Ferry and a thatched cottage near the Inn where Mr and Mrs Bottle lived with a schoolboy son. There was a very small one roomed cottage on the river bank where a Bob and Emma Keys lived. Another Bob Keys lived in a barge on the Creek, and Mr Tames lived in a hole in the ground on the boundary of the Murex factory.

"The Army brought some excitement to Rainham and at Ferry in the summer, rifle and gunshot being heard all day long. One firing position was right of Ferry Lane before Salamon's, and shots were fired across the lane. There would be two armed soldiers at Bendy Hook and the Halfway House to prevent accidents. All cattle were removed from the fields and lots of red flags flown.

"There was a farm at Coldharbour about a mile from the Ferry. Mr Blows was the farmer and he had no neighbours. A few farmworkers cottages had been vacated some years earlier and the remains, with the farm, must be buried under the waste that has been dumped there over the years.

"There was very little traffic on Ferry Lane. As well as Salamon's tanker truck, Murex had two steam wagons, a Foden and a Sentinel and, of course, a manager's car. The Three Crowns had a Romford Brewery delivery. A horse drawn cart collected household rubbish. Chandler's Bakers delivered milk and newspapers in their van. The postman and most workers at the factories used bicycles in the mid-20s.

"Stephens started a local bus service, but only when required. The first 'bus' was an open truck with boxes for seats and another box to make access easier. Edwards concentrated on the village and smallholdings area. Rainham Ferry had no gas, electricity, water or sewage. Factories had their own wells and water for home use was collected in pails. The Three Crowns had a 10 gallon tank on wheels and water was collected from Field's. White's, the barge repairers and builders had a yard beside the Public House employing six people, who were responsible for all Salamon's barge repairs and barge building.

"Yes - Ferry Lane was peaceful then!"

The Ferry area was bustling on summer weekends and holidays when it became a seaside resort, offering teas, boat trips and ferry rides across the river to Erith. The children enjoyed their sticks of Rainham Ferry rock. A Linney wrote in *Peepshow of the Port of London* in 1923, 'undoubtedly the pleasantest spot along the river described in these pages is at Rainham'. Daily newspapers advertised 'A day by the river at Rainham Ferry', and this resulted in many people from the East End of London visiting during the summer. A bus service ran from Oxford Street on weekdays and Wormwood Scrubs on Sundays, and passengers would alight for a ride or walk to the river. Edwards and Stephens private coaches or even converted lorries carried passengers along Ferry Lane

Murex Ltd., who came here in 1917, gradually absorbed the entire area, including the Three Crowns. In later years Murex was taken over by British Oxygen (B.O.C.), the entire site was demolished in 1999.

Many of the top London Hotels (Ritz, Savoy, Dorchester, etc.) and the Bank of England would dump their silver, brass, or epns salvers, tureens, cutlery, etc. at Cunis's Shoot before it was developed. My Granddad worked here for several years. Workers would keep the smaller pieces by for their homes, or would bring them home, crush them, and when they had a sack full of 'tots' would weigh them in for the cash.

J C Fields, candle and soap manufacturers, had a factory in Ferry Lane from 1906 to 1937. Many years ago a local lady told me she had worked there making mothballs and would often tuck a few in the tops of her black lisle stockings for the wardrobe at home. "Perks of the job," she said proudly.

Barge Cottage, next to the Three Crowns.
Walter and Bet Wisbey once lived here before moving to Melville Road
Walter tended the horses and his wife was the maid at the Farm at the Ferry

CHAPTER SEVEN

MEMORIES

As a small child I listened avidly to the reminiscences of my Mum and Gran. My Mum, Alice, born 1908, always told me not to hold romantic notions of the old days - times were hard and anything but romantic, as her story shows:- "My earliest memories began when I was about 4 years old in 1912. My Grandfather 'Old' Ben Hockley worked as a farm labourer for Poupart. He married Eliza Johnson whose father, known as 'Moley' Johnson was a molecatcher. Moleskins were highly valued as they were used in plumbing and leadwork as well as for clothing. Grandfather Johnson always wore a moleskin waistcoat - his trademark, I suppose. Ben and Eliza moved into a cottage in Back Street where they had five children. My father, 'young' Ben, was born in 1880. When he was 11 he started work as a rook scarer on Poupart's Farm. He would throw stones at the birds as they landed to feed on the crops.

"By the time he was 18, Ben was cowman at Poupart's. It was at this time he met mother, Elizabeth Fitch. She was visiting her Granny at Eastbury Cottages, Barking, near the Harrow, where Ben - *en route* to Smithfield Market - was watering his horse and cattle at the municipal trough. Mum liked the look of him, so she skipped round his cart and gave the horse a carrot, hoping he would notice her. He did, of course, and arranged to meet her on her day off as she was 'in service'. They married a couple of years later.

"In 1914 Dad left Pouparts to work at Curtis's Farm in Berwick Pond Road, and having to vacate his tied cottage, rented one of Tommy Young's houses at 65 Melville Road, known as brass knocker row, but at the onset of the Great War the cherished brass knockers and ornate railings were removed and melted down for munitions.

"I remember the day we moved to the Village. The cart was laden with our possessions, Mum and my sister, Jessie, who was holding our cat named Min, sat at the front of the cart with the driver. My Dad walked, carrying me on his shoulders - a flying angel he called it. The War had just broken out and as we approached Dover's Corner there was a lot of activity. A German plane had come down in the field near The Albion and the airman had, miraculously, scrambled from the wreckage, only to face a group of angry men armed with cudgels and pitchforks. I saw all this from my father's shoulders.

"After we moved Mum took in washing for the Gunary family. I would walk to their farm at Wennington and back carrying a huge wicker basket full of laundry, I had to stop several times as it was so heavy. Mum did the washing in the copper and put it through the mangle. My job was the ironing using a heavy iron, which was heated on the kitchener. One day she put the fingers of her left hand through the mangle. I wrapped her hand in a wet cloth and walked her to Dr Danaher's at the corner of Melville Road. When he unwrapped the cloth I passed clean out at the sight of her poor crushed and bleeding fingers.

"My Granddad 'Old' Ben, by then a widower, called at our cottage each evening for his tea. I loved him so, he always sat me on his knee and would give me an apple or a handful of woodnuts, depending on the season. Once he brought home one of the many farmyard kittens. He took it out of his pocket, put it on the floor and it ran straight up the curtain and crouched under the pelmet. It was really wild and took us a long time to tame it.

"When I left school I went into service at Hewitt's, owners of the Short Blue Fishing Line, who had moved the business from Barking to Great Yarmouth by this time, but the older members of the family remained at Barking where I worked. (The Barking Smack public house at Yarmouth was named for the Short Blue Fishing Line, as was The Short Blue in Barking). After a time I got homesick, came back to Rainham and got a job at Jurgen's Margarine Factory at Purfleet, where many Rainham people worked. We all met at the Station and, when we alighted from the train, a man would set the pace and we all fell in step with him, arriving just in time to clock in and position ourselves at our workstations. I worked with another 16 year old girl, called Hilda, who was to remain a lifelong friend. A few years on, my Mum got Hilda a job as Mrs Gunary's companion. Occasionally we were lowered into the huge steel vats that held the margarine, to clean them out. We would tie mutton cloths around our feet and elbows and waltz around the drum singing, not realizing that our voices echoed all over the dairyroom.

"I met my husband, Ted, in 1924 at a dance at the Garrison, Purfleet, where he was Master of Ceremonies. I had to leave work when we married in 1927, as married women weren't expected to work in those days.

"After his retirement from the farm around 1950, my Dad got a job as a grave digger at the Jews' Cemetery. On his first day Mr Soloman's asked him to help lift a corpse from a coffin so that the Jewish ladies could wash and lay it out. Not knowing that *rigor mortis* was only a temporary state - the body in question having returned to its former suppleness - Dad ran all the way home and said, "They're burying them up there afore they're dead," and vowed never to return. Needless to say he was back the next morning as he needed the pay."

The pictures above are of Ted, aged 20, and Alice, aged 16.

Violet, now in her nineties, tells a little of her eventful life:- "I was born in Blewitts Cottages in 1907. When I was 5 I went to South Hornchurch School in Blacksmiths Lane. Mrs Purkiss had the general store at the Cherry Tree Lane end of Blewitts, I used to call there on my way to school to buy a bar of chocolate to eat with a biscuit for my lunch. A few years on and I would serve in the shop after school and at weekends.

"When I left school I worked as a nanny to Florrie Tabard whose parents ran the Cauliflower. I had to sleep with Florrie, who had the annoying habit of rubbing my earlobes until she drifted off to sleep: it's a wonder they don't reach my shoulders. After a while I got fed up with this and found myself a job at the Sterling Works in Dagenham, making coil springs for wirelesses. This was intricate work which caused me eyestrain, so I went over to cabinet assembly. I was later made redundant, so I went to work at Jurgen's at Purfleet. My job was packing the margarine and butter. I would laugh to myself as I packed the same butter into all the different packets – each manufacturer claiming that their product was superior.

On the left this lovely snapshot taken in the 1920s shows Irene Bullock, prior to her marriage to Bill Polly, with her parents. Her brother and sister-in-law were holding up the blanket, in order to hide the mangle and the tin baths on the cottage wall.

"I left in 1929 to get married, you weren't actually sacked, but companies didn't employ married women in those days, so you knew you had to give your notice in. After my marriage to Bill I moved into 12 Melville Road where I lived for about 10 years.

"I was on holiday in Margate with my husband and 6 year old daughter, Stella, when war broke out. It felt very weird coming home on the coach in the blackout. The next morning, a Sunday, I was giving Stella her wash at the kitchen sink when we had the first air raid. Mr Biggs' son was sittting on the window ledge of his house in Cowper Road (which backed on to mine) when his and several other houses, were bombed. It was a miracle he survived. There were many miracles during the war. My house had a crack down the back wall that you could put your hands into. We were supposed to move to a house in Grangewood Avenue and picked up the keys. Bill and his Dad brought the shovels with them to build a shelter. Bill's Dad went upstairs and quickly came down saying, "Come on, you're not staying here, it's running alive with bugs, and they've been keeping chickens in one of the bedrooms." As we were on our way home an airman was trying to land his plane safely. It was so close you could see him motioning to us to get out of the way. We were so upset when his plane crashed near Ingrebourne Road. Soon after this we moved to Eastwood Drive, where a doodlebug (flying bomb) hit a pylon which crashed into the newly built bungalows. They were rebuilt after the war!

"I still live in Eastwood Drive and have many happy memories of my 63 years here."

Alice and Iris Collis in their dug-out in East Close

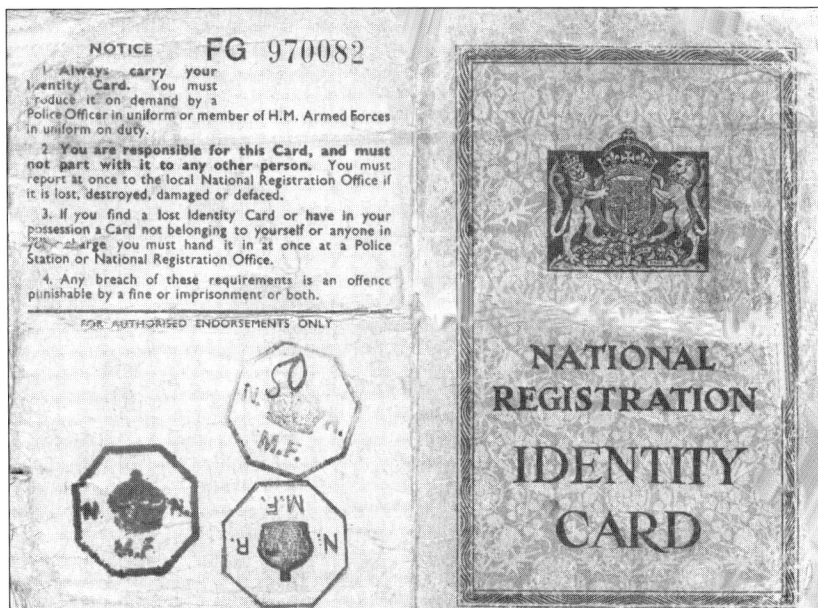

A (slightly battered) Identity Card

CHAPTER EIGHT

THE WAR YEARS

During the war most commodities were rationed. One person's allowance for an average week in 1941 was:-

Bacon and ham	4 ozs.	Cooking fats	8 ozs
Sugar	8 ozs.	Butter	2 ozs
Meat (rationed by price)	1/- (5p)	Tea	2 ozs

Plus 16 points per month for other rationed foods, subject to availability.

In July 1941 domestic users were restricted to 1 ton of coal a month. Patriotic Britons were urged not to exceed more than 5 inches of hot water in their baths. Soap rationing came into effect in February, 1942, with each person being allocated 3 ozs. of toilet soap a month.

Utility clothing was introduced in 1942, designed with an eye to economising on raw materials. The finished look of the garment was unimportant. Pleats and flounces went out of fashion by government demand, hemlines were raised and double-breasted coats were banned.

The photograph is of Ted and Alice Collis, who is looking very chic in her single breasted collarless coat, made by her own fair hand.

These Murex workers and friends enjoy a day on the town in 1942. Pictured left to right:- Back row: Ann Stringer, Joyce Felton, Betty Hogg, Iris Collis, Alice Collis, Emm McGhee. Front row: ? Lock, Dollie Hogg, Ann Fordham, Lydia Brewster, Lucy Turner, Paddy Smith, with Florrie Hogg in the corner.

My sister, Iris, was born in 1928. She attended Pitman's College in Forest Gate, leaving at 14 to start work at Lloyd's Shipping Office in the City of London. Here are her recollections of the war years:-

.   "I was born in Brights Avenue, but we moved to 14 East Close when I was about 6. When war came Dad was in the Army and Mum worked at the munitions factory in Ferry Lane. She was a great needlewoman and would make swagger coats and men's dressing gowns from American army blankets, which were wonderful quality and not a bit itchy. The army camp was in Warwick Lane, not far from the Berwick and Launders cross-roads.

Mum also made wedding gowns from parachute silk - each was made from 65 yards of the finest quality silk. I remember a pilot coming down on land near Glebe Road. Several women rushed towards him, not to help him, just to relieve him of his parachute. Phyllis Kulik (née Collis) is wearing one of Mum's parachute silk gowns.

"When the siren went off we all made for the air raid shelters or dugouts in our back gardens. We would just get settled when a cat from down the road would come to the opening and mark his territory. I was going to kill that cat! One day I finally caught him and handed him to Mum. "I don't want it, you was the one as was going to kill it!", she said. I couldn't do it, of course, so I let him go. Needless to say he was back the next night.

35

This shelter can still be seen in Mr. Cook's garden in Parsonage Road.

One time we ran for the shelter and Gran tripped and her false teeth fell out. We forgot about the bombs as we grappled about in the snow to find them. Oh, no! Hitler wasn't going to catch her with no teeth in! I remember Mum shouting, "Come on, they're dropping bombs, not sandwiches!"

On the site of the Old Smithy opposite the Working Men's Club, a hut was erected for the Air Raid Patrol.

A R P Wardens: Mr Bullen, Mr Cook, three un-named. Sitting on left Miss Edwards

Iris's friend, Jean, had sadder memories of the war:- "I was born and lived in Rainham, which was just a village at the outbreak of war, when I was 10 years old. A number of people of foreign extraction, including a Norwegian family, were dispersed from Rainham as it was classed as a restricted area. Hornchurch Aerodrome was just a few fields away, there was an army camp at White Post Corner and, at Purfleet 2 miles or so away - there was a prisoner of war camp and rifle ranges. There were, of course, ranges at Rainham .

Promoting 'War Bonds' outside the A.R.P. Hut in Upminster Road South
Third from right is Miss Croot (later Mrs Vinton): 3rd from left Mr Cook

"German aircraft followed the River Thames and, considering how small the village was, we were heavily bombed. My brother was at band practice when a lot of incendiary bombs fell in the main road. We spent many nights for many months in the air raid shelters as our road was near the A13. The pom pom guns went back and forth during the night.

"One particular incident recalls a poignant memory. It was a Saturday afternoon and one of our lads was trying to return safely to the Aerodrome. His aircraft was in trouble, but he managed to steer it over the allotment, which was bordered by the houses of Ingrebourne and Melville Roads. Sadly the aircraft crashed and he was killed.

"My husband's family were bombed by landmines and two friends of my mother and a lad from our school were killed. Rainham School was closed at this time and one of the bedrooms at 39 Ingrebourne Road was used as a classroom.

"My father, a carpenter, worked at the docks repairing pontoons and motor torpedo boats. Once he was sent to do a temporary repair to the House of Lords which had been bombed. He would then come home and do fire duty.

"Once the blitz started we were bombed continuously, and were eventually evacuated to relatives in Scotland. I remember our journey through London to King's Cross, the fire fighters with their hose pipes, brave men and women trying to rescue folk from the previous nights bombing. As much as we hated the claustrophobic fear of the shelters, my brother and I were terrified of leaving our Mum and Dad."

End of war celebrations in Grangewood Avenue. Jean Elsdon (née Pringle) is standing on the right of the picture. Edith, wife of Councillor Holmes, is on left holding a plate of sandwiches. Homestead Nurseries is at the rear of the picture.

Irene remembers her time in the Girls' Training Corps:- "At the age of 15 I saw a notice stating that a company of the GTC was being formed, so I and my sister Joyce decided to join. We were based in the junior school, later demolished by incendiary bombs. We had to supply our own uniforms, of white blouse, black tie, forage cap, navy skirt and dark stockings. Later we added navy blue battledress jackets. We started off by taking a first aid course, and were instructed by two air raid wardens. They were very good, I still remember quite a lot of what they taught us and have used it on several occasions. We were trained in marching, saluting and semaphore - which we enjoyed. We had Church parades, attended British Legion Services at the War Memorial and took part in the carnival.

Girls' Training Corps, 1944

"In 1944 the Home Guard asked our officers if any girls would like to transfer to them as telephone operators. I said I would like to try, was made up to sergeant and given a section of girls. I had to make out a rota for the girls to man the telephones at the Home Guard headquarters above a builders' shop next to the police station on the old A13. We had three other telephones manned by the girls, The Lodge in the Jews' Cemetery, over an empty shop in Southend Road and the derelict Wennington House (Kent View, now stands on this site).

"One night a week we used a small tennis pavilion, still standing in the back garden of 5 Arterial Avenue, for morse code training. We also had a session one Sunday morning on a small rifle range in the corner of the Jews' Cemetery, under the instruction of Lieutenant Rivers. Not long after this the Home Guard were stood down, but I am very proud of the Certificate of Appreciation I received for 'doing my bit' in the war."

ERNIE'S WARTIME MEMORIES.

Ernie Cook, 82, can remember war being declared when he was 18 years old, and working in a metal factory. He and his mother would go down to the Anderson shelter at the bottom of his garden in Parsonage Road during air raids, while his father, an Air Raid Precautions worker, would go out on duty.

Ernie and his mother would talk, play cards and listen to the wireless, providing the enemy had not jammed the broadcasts, as they often did.

"The dog was always the first one down there. The atmosphere was extremely damp and claustrophobic," said Ernie, a retired engineer. "There were bunk beds on each side, with a shelf and small stove in the middle for making tea - and that was it."

Ernie can remember shouting to the neighbours over the garden fence as they walked down to the shelter, saying to each other, "Here we go again."

"You would get very blasé about going down there as time went on," said Ernie. "I remember when a land mine went off at the bottom of our street and killed eight people. That was very scary. We were in the house at the time and ran out to help rescue people who were trapped tinder the rubble."

Ernie and his wife Mary moved back to the house in 1958, and generously open their home once a year to let children from Parsonage Farm Junior School come to see how people used to live during the war. Mary talks to the children at the top of the garden, while Ernie takes a few of them down at a time to show them the shelter, and answers their questions.

"We don't use it for anything now, although my mother always said what a brilliant pantry it made when the war was finished," Ernie added.

LILLI'S STORY
Evalda, known as Lilli, was born in Faornole, Italy, in 1927. She recalls her early years in this tiny mountain top village, and the events that led to her coming to Rainham:- "I lived in a remote village, with no toilet or water supply to our house. One of my brothers had been killed in the war, the other was missing in action. We used to say Mum had tears in her pocket as she often cried, wondering what would happen to me. I told her not to worry, I was going to become a nun. Every week I would walk five miles to a little church where there was a Nunnery

and Orphanage. Four nuns worked a piece of ground given to them by a local farmer, who then sold the produce for them. I would help by playing with the children.

"When we needed to go to the toilet we went in pairs. I would knock for the girl next door as we had to go into the bushes and had to have a lookout in case someone else wanted to use the same bush. The village water supply was from two taps half a mile from our house and there was usually a queue. One day there was a lot of confusion, British and American soldiers of the Eighth Army were in the village. On Sunday I went to get water and a young British soldier asked if I knew anyone who could wash his clothes for him. My friend from next door was with me and it was arranged that he would call at her house with the washing. However, Jimmy called at my house instead, and said the washing had only been an excuse, as he wanted to get to know me. Mum apologized that she had no food to offer him, we couldn't speak each others' language, but made ourselves understood.

"He then called each day bringing chocolate or sugar cubes. Mum would sit by the front door with them in her apron and give one to each child who passed. We'd never known such times. He brought porridge, which we ate with hot water and salt, then jelly crystals that we sprinkled in water and drank. We didn't have any idea how to use these things, they were unknown to us. His Sergeant, a Scotsman, would leave a tin of pears on the table outside our house, we would soak our bread in the juice and eat it with the fruit.

"When Jimmy asked if he could marry me it was a shock as we hadn't even kissed. Mum agreed and Jim gave her the box of candles he had brought I was worried who would look after my parents and said I couldn't possible leave them. His unit moved on and I thought that was the last I'd seen of him.

Some weeks later Jimmy returned, he had applied for permission for us to marry. An Army Officer called round each Sunday with an interpreter, and after nine months they decided I was respectable and, with a reference from my Priest and Doctor, permission was granted. The Doctor who lived six miles away didn't really know me as we could never afford a visit from him. Mum cured us from all ailments by boiling herbs and giving us the water to drink. If the Doctor did visit the village all the children would run out just to look at his car, which was nothing more than a box on wheels, but it was wonderful to us.

"Jimmy had to become a Catholic to marry me. One of the sisters of our Priest said, "He must love you very much to change his religion for you." I hadn't realized; I thought the whole world was Catholic. A neighbour made my wedding dress from fabric Jimmy bought, he also paid for my shoes and a bunch of lilies. We left for England and had two weeks honeymoon in Rome, *en route*, where our marriage was blessed by the Pope. We stayed with a family who insisted on seeing our marriage certificate first

"I arrived in England in June, 1946, two months after I left my village, as I had to stay in Austria until there were enough soldiers' wives to fill the train. An Officer handed me over to Jimmy; I felt like a market animal. My mother-in-law rushed over and embraced me. When we got to her flat there was a banner across the hall saying, "Welcome home Lilli." I thought I had married Churchill's son, or someone equally important. There was lino (I'd never seen this as our floor was brick at home), a carpet runner and armchairs, I'd never seen such luxury.

"I had a terrible time with the language as I didn't understand English, and felt so alone when Jimmy went to work with his father, although we were living with his parents and sister. One day I was at home when a woman visited. There was such a fuss, kissing and cuddling.

When she left my sister-in-law said, "That was our cousin. It would be so nice if you could greet Jimmy with the words, 'Jimmy your cousin came today'." I repeated the words to myself for hours and when he came home rushed to the door excitedly and said "Jimmy, you are a cow son." It took a lot of explaining before they all fell about laughing. Another time I wanted to be independent and do my own shopping, so I went to the Co-op to buy Jimmy some underpants. The male assistant sniggered when I asked for two knickers for my husband. When I cooked the roast I put a whole apple in the centre of each plate, I'd heard something about pork and apple sauce.

"Jimmy worked for Bergers in Hackney, but the business moved to Selinas Lane, Dagenham, and the travelling was too much, so we decided to move to Rainham. We took out a mortgage on our house in Findon Gardens, which cost £1,800 in 1956. I was so happy, even though we had no furniture, just a utility mattress which sagged through the springs of the bed so that our backs touched the floor. We saved and later bought a bedroom suite from Times Furnishing for £101.

"I worked as an outdoor machinist for Janice Lee Gowns of Lambs Lane, and was paid 1/6d per garment . If there were lots of frills or pockets I got 2/- (10p). I used to buy remnants of fabric from the market to make my girls dresses and managed to put away 10/- (50p) a week for them, so they had £50 each when they started work.

"I have lived in Rainham for 45 years now and have made many friends and enjoyed a happy life here with my husband and family. My eldest daughter, Maria, went to visit my Mother in Italy in the 1960s, fell in love and married there. She now teaches English at a college there. I tell her, "You take care of my country, and I'll take care of yours."

ARTHUR'S STORY

During the war Arthur worked at Rainham Lodge Farm in Berwick Pond Road, and had to take the horses from there to Poupart's Farm in Rainham Road and Cherry Tree Lane. He would take a short cut through La Salette Church grounds, the horses clip-clopping over the cobbles. Quite often he was confronted by a nun who would request, "Can't you make the horses walk quietly as we have a service in progress."

He also remembers the smogs, known as 'pea soupers' - thick fog caused by a combination of fog and smoke from coal fires - when several of the farmhands would sneak across the road to the Albion for a quick pint.

Rainham Lodge Farm, the home of the diplomat, Baron William Strang, was later demolished, the land being divided by Essex Council into five smaller farms. The Lodge had been used after the war as a meeting place for Canadian soldiers on manoeuvres. Turners now have three farms and Chapmans, who have a market garden stall in Romford Market, the other two. Fred Croot had a radio and cycle shop opposite Rainham Primary School (now a printers). He used to charge up accumulators, which were used to drive valve sets for radios.

ALF'S STORY

This note from Alf recalls:- "After watching the Battle of Britain on T.V., I was reminded of my experience during this period.

"I was working as a saw doctor at Thames Plywood Manufacturers at Barking when war was declared. This being a reserved occupation, I joined the Home Guard. We had to patrol from the Princess, Dagenham, where we reported for duty, to the War Memorial, Rainham - about 2 miles. The factory kept going 24 hours a day as plywood was used for assault barges, railway carriages and floors for the Spitfires. We also made propellers. Some of the knives used for production weighed 3 cwt, others needed two men to lift just one. I constantly had a supply of knives and saws to service so I was never finished work. When everyone went to the shelter I foolishly remained working. If a bomb had dropped nearby I would not be writing this narrative I am now 88."

JOAN'S STORY

Here, Joan shares her memories of Rainham:- "Having lived in Rainham since 1939, I have seen many changes. My earliest memories are of air raids, air raid warnings, gas masks and Vls, the dreaded 'doodlebugs'. Despite all this, life went on. We went to school as usual, going in the air raid shelters if there was a raid. There was only one school in the Village area then, and the infants, juniors and seniors used it. Now there are three more in this part of Rainham, so you can see how much it has grown over the years.

"After the war, although we did not have the televisions, videos and computers that the children have today, we had something money cannot buy - our freedom. We would be out all day during the weekends and school holidays, over Bluebell Woods, Abbey Woods and Spring Farm Park (Spring Farm as it was in the 1900s is on the left). We had park keepers (commonly known as 'parkies') to keep us in order, although the only 'crimes' we committed were knock down ginger or scrumping apples and pears from the gardens in Parsonage Road and all the other roads off Upminster Road North. These roads were not made up then, as most of the properties were no more than wooden huts. Gradually people bought plots of land and had their houses built, then the roads were eventually made up. Another favourite pastime was playing cowboys and Indians, or hide and seek, in the ruins of a large old house called The Hollies, which was between where Barclay's Bank and Parkway is now. At one time there was talk of building a cinema on the site, but it never materialised.

"When I started work in London as a shorthand typist in 1953, the steam trains were still running. Travelling to and from work in those days left a lot to be desired. It took as long to get to Barking in those days as it does to get to Fenchurch Street now. The entrance to the station which was a lovely old wooden building, was down by the side of the Phoenix Hotel. When the line was modernised a new station was built in Ferry Lane. As well as being an unreliable service, we had to put up with the awful 'smogs', that either made trains late or cancelled them altogether. It was not unusual to have to walk home from Barking, where the trains often terminated. And then there was the excuse of cows on the line!

"With the introduction of supermarkets, all the little friendly shops have closed down. When I was first married Friday was shopping day. Each shop you went in there was always a laugh and a joke, especially the butchers. He always had some joke or comment to make us laugh, and would flirt with all the ladies, no matter how old they were. You would always come home feeling cheerful; shopping in those days was like a tonic.

"All in all, although we have a better standard of living now, I think I prefer the times when we had a book and an orange in our Christmas stocking, and bread and jam for tea - and no television! I used to love listening to the radio, Paul Temple, Dick Barton, The Archers, Children's Hour and others too numerous to mention, kept us entertained for hours.

"Oh! For the simple life and Rainham as it used to be.

Rainham Fire Brigade

The first motor vehicle used by Murex

CHAPTER NINE

PEACE AT LAST

When the war ended life went on pretty much as before. People took a while to get used to peace once again, but looked forward to their family get togethers around the piano on Saturday evenings. Each person would sing or do a turn, everyone keeping to their own particular piece.

Mum and Iris would play Chopsticks on the piano. Gran would tell a ghost story, usually the *Mistletoe Bough*, about a wedding party in a stately home where the guests played hide and seek. The young bride hid in a heavy oak chest, her body lying undiscovered for many years. This story had the rapt attention of the youngsters, particularly when her lowered voice took on a sinister tone as she said, "She lay withering there in a living tomb."

The acts were varied, many a smile, many a tear ensued. Uncle Sid sang 'Brown boots' and we would all join in the chorus. Dad and Uncle Arthur would bring in a large square board and sprinkle it with sand, remove most of their clothes, put towels around their waists and tea towels on their heads and proceed to do an Egyptian sand dance. This was hilarious.

I can remember everyone failing about laughing as Granddad sat, po faced, on the settle singing about 'When Paddy stole the rope'. Sadly I can no longer remember the words and have been unable to trace them.

Alice and Coral Collis in the Park, 1954

Great-Grandma Alice, who kept an eye on the little ones, would sing them to sleep with her gentle lullaby.

Sadly, most evening these days are spent around the television.

ALF'S GAMES
Alf, born in 1912, remembers the games he used to play as a child:-
High Jimmy Knacker
This required two teams with 4 on one side and 5 on the other. A coin was tossed and the losing side would stand one of its members against a wall, facing away from same. The remainder of his side would bend forward creating a line of backs with the First boy touching the one standing (like leap frog). The opposing team would then go across the road, leap onto the backs of the other team and call, "Hi Jimmy Knacker, one, two three away." While this was being

called all the boys had to remain on the backs of the others. If a boy fell off then the other team were the ones to leap. The idea was for the first boy to leap on as far as possible, for if 5 boys a side were playing there were only four backs to leap on.

Gobs and Bonsters

This was our version of five stones.

Tippi Cat

This was a game for 3 to 4 boys. You needed a stick about 30" long, and a small one about 6 inches long. Two circles about 2 ft. in diameter were drawn on the ground with chalk in alignment with each other, the centre of each circle being about 3ft. apart. A coin was tossed to determine who would bat first, one boy would pitch while the other fielded. The lad who was in first had the long stick and the pitcher lobbed the small stick towards him, which the striker tried to hit. If he managed to strike whilst it was being fielded he placed the long stick alternatively in each circle counting at the same time. If he did not hit the stick and it went into the circle he was out and another took his place.

King of the Golden Apples

For this game you needed a younger lad, or someone who hadn't played before. He would be crowned King and we would all be his servants. Someone might buy him an ice cream, if we were flush, or give him something to gain his confidence. He then had to say, "Bring me my golden apples," whereupon he would be pelted with bad apples and oranges which had been discarded by the greengrocer.

Chariot Racing

A minimum of 8 to 10 players, (4 chariots, 4 drivers, Started and a Judge). One lad would get down on all fours, then the driver would hold his legs up so he was resting on his hands. We would all line up and the starter would signal the off. The first chariot to arrive at the end of the course was the winner, but you did your best to hamper your opponents by fair means or foul, like bumping into each other or getting in your opponents' way. Various antics caused many a laugh. A quiet road was essential but traffic usually only consisted of the odd horse and cart. Cigarette cards would be wagered on the result, which made the game more interesting.

MY STORY

I have lived in Rainham since my birth in 1947 and had a wonderful childhood growing up in, what was then, a country village, surrounded by my family and friends - many of whom still live here. On the left are my mother and me by the A13 in 1947. Maybe my memories will remind them of the happy, carefree days we spent during the 'Fifties and sixties'.

My sister and I would visit our Gran in Melville Road after Sunday School. Parby, our name for Granddad, would sit one side of the kitchener and his brother-in-law, 'Beadle', the other with his ferret Jess in his pocket and his little Jack Russell, Gyp, at his feet. They were a familiar sight on the marshes or the flood plains of the Ingrehourne, either rabbitting or catching eels.

George 'Beadle' Fitch, so named as years before he was Village Beadle in Barking, had been a bit of a lad in his young days. A circus came to Barking in the early 1900s and Beadle ran off with the lion tamer's wife - only to return home a few months later, tail between his legs. After this he worked as a steeplejack travelling all over the country. He would entertain us with stories of his travels on return to Gran's. He could neither read nor write and Gran would read his mail to him, occasionally asking him to 'make your mark', whereupon he would sign with a cross.

In the winter Gran would bring in two pints of 'ops (home brew), heat a poker in the grate and put it into the beer. As a treat I was allowed to suck the froth off Parby's pint. Gran would pour two glasses of parsnip or rhubarb wine for her and my sister. I was too young (about 6 at this time). Not to be outdone I would disappear into the larder and pour myself a drink, not knowing that it was liquid parraffin. It puzzled me that the little glass I used didn't seem to fit my mouth, some years later I realised I was using an antique eyebath!

Later on Gran would make a cup of tea. The best bit came when she read the leaves after the cups were drained. There was always a tall dark stranger, man on a horse and a letter from America. I would slip from my chair and under the long fringed chenille tablecloth that reached the floor. Soon they were chatting, completely forgetting me. One day they were discussing a lady who lived down our road, the conversation was so exciting I couldn't wait to get home to see my cousin who lived opposite. The next afternoon we visited the lady in question and asked to see her skeletons. "What are you on about?" she asked. I explained that my sister said she had some in her cupboard. I remember that thrashing well!

There was a copper in the scullery where Gran made lovely puddings. Raisin roly-poly was my favourite, we would eat it hot spread with butter and sugar - it was delicious. Every week Beadle would bring home some eels for Gran to stew. I hated to see her chop them up, all the pieces would jump about on the draining board.

She also made brawn from a pig's head. One of my cousins would sneak an eye into his pocket and take it to school where he would pop it down the neck of the girl sitting in front of him in class. Boys were hateful they often got a chicken's foot and would sneak up behind you, place it on your shoulder and pull the sinews to draw the claws in which would scratch you. We would scream and they would laugh their heads off

The toilet at Gran's was in the back yard. We would have to cut toilet paper from squares of last week's newspapers and thread them on to a piece of string to hang by the loo, no Andrex in those days. Sometimes part of a headline caught your eye but it wasn't worth reading as you never got to the end of the story. There were no bathrooms in the cottages then, the tin baths, in two sizes, generally hung on the outside wall.

There was a hutch with two rabbits who would occasionally go missing, soon being replaced by much younger buns who, in turn, would also go missing. When asked their whereabouts Gran would say, "Oh! A fox probably run off with them." I had such a lovely picture in my mind of them all skipping over the fields together when, in actual fact, they were in a stew.

There was a chicken run in the garden - it was so lovely to put your hand in the warm straw and bring out an egg for breakfast the next morning. Most families had chicken runs then.

One evening our dog appeared with a cockerel in his mouth. It was a Rhode Island Red and Mum recognised it as belonging to Marge next door. She took the bird and crawled down the yard and into the next garden where she propped it up against the fence so it still looked alive. Our Bonzo was always in trouble, even the baker and milkman wouldn't deliver to us if he was in the front garden.

When I was 4 I became ill and was taken to St. Mary's Hospital, Paddington, where I was to stay for the next ten months. I was never told the nature of my illness - my sister used to refer to it as 'the dreaded lurgey'. After an operation I was transferred to the Ogilvy School of Recovery at Holland on Sea, where I stayed until mid-September, 1953. I hated being away from my family, and the only happy time I remember was the party we had to celebrate the Coronation of Elizabeth II (see picture on page 25).

When I returned home there was no place for me at Rainham Village School, so I went to Wennington. There were only 23 children, aged from 5 to 11, in the entire school of just one classroom. P.E. lessons were taken in 'The Hut', a wooden building replaced by the current Village Hall in the 1960s. During the summer our lessons were taken outdoors, either in Wennington churchyard, or one of the fields, where we sketched wild flowers for our nature study class.

Mr Taylor, who lived in the bungalow on the corner of The Green, was the headmaster; his wife headmistress. Another teacher, Miss White, cycled from Hornchurch each day. At lunchtimes we would all go to the scullery and pass our plates to Mrs Taylor who, wearing a wrapover floral pinafore, would serve our meal, assisted by Mrs Clarke. I caught the bus to school from my home in Ellis Avenue, but often walked home to save the penny-ha'penny bus fare. I would spend this on a penny bag of crisps, which were nothing more than a handful of greasy crumbs, and four blackjacks from Carringtons off licence on the corner of Brookway. This was at the end of a small parade of shops which included John's Green-grocers, Maison Yvonne ladies' hairdressers, Redding's grocery store and Molson's sweetshop.

In 1953 when I was 8, Mum decided I should have piano lessons. Mr Cook, the Church organist and choirmaster, a small elderly man who wore glasses with lens as thick as the bottom of milk bottles, arrived for my first lesson in our front room. Very impatient, he jabbed my fingers with a tuning fork each time I struck a wrong note. The lesson seemed to last for hours. When it was finished I turned off the light and shut the door, thinking he had gone through the French doors to the lounge. Mum investigated when she heard a thud and heard him groping about in the dark trying to find the door. My legs stung a little more than usual that night but it was worth it, he never returned and I was never to play a note.

I visited Gran daily during my school lunch hour. First, I would pick up the money and list from Aunt Zilph's house in Wennington Road. She sat in the bay window at an industrial sewing machine and never had time to speak as she was on piecework. There was always a 3d. piece waiting for me on my return - I usually bought a Dickie Bird's banana lolly at The Don in Wennington Road.

I would knock at the old lady's next to the Chapel alley, who always had a quarter of winter mixture and a tin of Kit-e-kat, then I would get Gran's list and cut through the Gospel Hall alley to Green's Stores in Wennington Road. One day a fence closed off the alley, the woman had got fed up with people passing her garden and the Chapel agents had given in to her constant complaints, which meant that I had to go the long way round. After that I would eat one of the sweets just to punish her.

In the 1950s most of the local children would play around The Hollies, an old house, which had been partially demolished and was in a state of dereliction, after school and during the holidays. Access was gained through a hole in the fence behind Rainham Rec. We were warned by our parents not to go there as there was a risk of falling masonry, but like most children didn't listen as we knew best. Fortunately apart from a few thorns and scraped shins no accidents occurred. However, I would get a slap across the back of my legs - usually with a wet cloth on my return home. I wondered how Mum knew where I'd been, not realising that the sticky buds on my ankle socks gave me away.

Each Saturday morning I was sent to Mayhew's for the weekend joint. I would recite the request, "Half a leg of lamb, about 8/6d, please John," all the way to the shop. Mum said to be polite as when she was young old Mr Mayhew would refuse to serve anyone he considered impolite. When buying liver you had to take a plate with you as Mr M thought it quite improper to wrap offal. The business had been in the Mayhew family for years, passing from father to son. In the early 1960s John Mayhew sadly took his own life on the premises which stood empty until its demolition in 1964.

When I was about eight I became responsible for collecting the 'Foresters' money each month from my many relatives. I had to take it to the local agent, old 'Ummer' Ellis in Ingrebourne Road. His real name was Harry, but as his conversation was interspersed with 'um, er,' it had earned him his unfortunate nickname.

An Ancient Order of Foresters Dinner/Dance, 1961
Front row (l to r): ?: Wyn Turner, Alice Collis, ?: Back: Mick Turner, ?, Ted Collis,?,?

The Ancient Order of Foresters was a 'Friendly Society', and its many functions were to provide savings, loans, mortgages, etc. They held annual outings and Dinners and Dances for their members, presided over by the appointed Chief Ranger. Many local people belonged either to the Foresters, or their rivals, The Oddfellows.

THE SHEPHERD

Jock Milne of Wennington Road tended the sheep on the marshes for 55 years. I had spent an afternoon with him and he told me a little of his life as Rainham's shepherd:-

"I left school when I was fourteen and a half and started my working life as a shepherd. My parents had a small farm at Premney, Aberdeenshire, so I did have a little knowledge of sheep. My first task was to cycle for two days to Laurancekirk to pick up 400 sheep. It took seven days on the road with them to get back to Aberdeen.

"A few years later a man from Hainault Farm came to Aberdeen to buy sheep. I was earning £1 a week at this time. He offered me a job on Rainham Marshes for the princely sum of £2.05p. I thought I was on my way to becoming a millionaire (Hainault Farm had sheep in the forest as well as on Rainham Marshes). I arrived in Rainham on 4th May, 1937.

"The sheep were grazed on the marsh between April and October. We had to take them off for the winter as it was Ministry of Defence land and that was their rules. When war started we grazed them throughout the year, plus I had a Land Army girl called Margaret to help me then. Mayhews also grazed sheep on the rifle ranges. The downfall of the marshes came with the construction of the silt lagoons.

"Eventually the Fresh Meat Co. of Smithfield took over the marsh, but later I tendered for it and had it to myself for the 11 years prior to my retirement. I built myself a series of sheds which I named 10 Downing Street, one of them contained a bed and a gas cooker as during lambing I had to be there 24 hours a day. My usual working week was from dawn to dusk 7 days a week. My border collies, Spark and Moss, my faithful companions. My wife spent a lot of time with me and would wind the wool ready for packing into sacks. I used to get 2/6d. for each sheep I sheared.

'10 Downing Street'

"There were 290 acres of Port of London Authority land, plus another 460 acres with another 230 acres on the rifle ranges. There were well over 1,000 sheep and, of course, the numbers grew with each lambing.

"There were 5 or 6 marshmen employed by the M.o.D. to maintain the ditches and fences and, quite often, several poachers after the many rabbits that abounded there. Watercress grew abundantly and the ditches were full of eels.

"I had an old horse and cart. My young daughter, Carol, would carry a brick with her on each journey and bang it on the front of the cart to make the horse walk a bit faster. I used to take him into the Village to be shoed at the Blacksmiths opposite the Working Men's Club. When the smith closed it became a Regent Garage, later a Jet petrol station came in its place, a sign of the times. I then progressed to a pickup truck in which I would take 8 sheep each week to Chelmsford Market. In the 1950s £5 of petrol would take me to Chelmsford and back twice. I retired from the marsh in October, 1992."

THE CONCRETE BARGES

A familiar sight on the foreshore of the Thames are the old concrete barges, built by Covences at Cunis's Jetty. Large lagoons were constructed and the barges were built and floated into the Thames. They were originally intended for use as part of the Mulberry Harbour, but as soon as they made contact with each other they broke, and were 'dumped' at Rainham at the request of the Port of London Authority. It was rumoured that they were used at Arromanches, Normandy, during the D-Day landings, a much more romantic notion, but in fact they have never been further down the Thames than their current site.

Mr Tweed, who had a business at Layer-de-la-Hay, Essex, came to live on one of these barges, which he named *Thatcher's Barge*. He constructed a shed on the deck, plus a sign saying 'Layer Shipping Company'. There was even a small garden and washing line. Access to the living quarters was via the hatch where the interior was carpeted and comfortably furnished. He made a living from selling driftwood which had been washed up on to the shore.

In 1981 Mr & Mrs Milne were invited to a dinner party on the barge. The invitation gives us an insight into the unique personality of Mr Tweed.

Shelley*and Hugh Knevitt.

Out of Capetown SA via South and North America . . . .

_____

H S Tweed requests the pleasure of the company of:-

Mr & Mrs Milne.

At a modest dinnah party in honour of the above to be given on Thatcher's Barge, off Wennington Marshes, Rainham Essex. Friday May 15th 1981.

6.45 for 7.15 pm:

Evening dress optional.

(not recommended)

Hand-rail fitted to gang-plank for the occasion.

* The birthday girl.

MENU.

Prawn Cocktail, or Soup of the day.

Lemon,orange, blackcurrant, pineapple.

Mixed grille.

Mushroms, bacon, liver, eggs, sausage, mashed potatoes, wild spinach,petit-poids sweet-corn.

Choice flavours of jelly (on a plate) cream, South African pears, peaches or apricots.

English Cheddar, Stilton, Camembert and Crackers.

Coffee, tea, fruit drink.

Water by Colchester water Co
Sherry by English importers.
Rug by Joyce and Co.
Gas by Calor (Hopefully, By kind permission of the vandals?)
Wild spinach by courtesy Port of London Authority.
Chairs by Jock Milne (the Shepherd).
Plates by B of E.

Hon: Catering Manager, Roast Master and Mousse Taster. Felix Thatcher.

Plates by B of E - possibly ex-Bank of England from Cunis's Shoot.

Felix Thatcher was his cat

One day each week Mr Tweed, smartly dressed and carrying a briefcase, would go off to London on business. Sadly, one day his body was found in the river. It was assumed that he had slipped from the gangplank, which ran to his barge from the sea wall.

CHAPTER TEN

SPORT & LEISURE

Foresters' Ladies' Day Outing, about 1914
3rd from left, front row, Mrs Sawkins: the old lady seated in charabanc is Gert Ellis

Ladies' outings were quite rare around this time. The men had annual outings, usually organized by the pubs or clubs. As the charabanc departed the wives would waive them off and the children would run behind the coach shouting, "Throw out your mouldies", then grapple in the dirt for the farthings and halfpennies which had been thrown into the road.

In 1939 a Rainham cinema company bought the site previously occupied by The Hollies, intending to build a cinema. The name proposed was the Isis. After the war a license could not be obtained and the project was finally abandoned in 1958. Some years earlier, in 1936, a banner across the Vicarage announced its replacement by a cinema. Thankfully, nothing came of this scheme.

Street party in Ingrebourne Road to celebrate the Jubilee, 1935

This snapshot was taken outside the Grangewood Café 1936/7
Back row :? Fred Clarke ? Seated Jacky Deeks, Ernie Cook, ? Front row: Arthur Pimm.
Background right is the new Police Station

Putting by the A13 in 1937
There was a putting green by the Café, and a pavillion at the rear.
The pavilion can still be seen as it is in the garden of a property in Arterial Avenue

Rainham Carnival Court, 1938
Pictured left to right: Maid of honour Joan Valentine, flower girl Jean Burgess, ?, Norman Wright ?
page boy Ronald Scott and Queen Vera Keeble

Carnival day 1950. The ladies in the foreground are wearing 'turbans' made from headscarves, a fashion started during WW2 by Land Army girls, and carried on after the war by factory workers and housewives.

Quite often they would be wearing hair curlers beneath the snoods

'Birdie', daughter of F P Hill

The sandpit between Melville and Ingrebourne Roads was a well loved recreation area in the 1930s, as this snapshot of Iris Collis and her baby cousin Barbara Cottrell shows

RAINHAM WORKING MEN'S CLUB

On 14th September, 1920, there was a meeting arranged by T Hounslow at Rainham School to discuss the opening of a Club. Several men attended and W J Montgomery was appointed Chairman and R Clark as Secretary and the names of those present were taken who were in favour of a Club. The next business was to find a piece of ground suitable at the next meeting on 10th November, when Mr Clark had to resign from pressure of work and C Widows took his place. Between the meetings it had been discovered that Mr Blows was willing to sell a suitable piece of land for £120 and that Mr Mason had found huts at Purfleet for sale at £50 each. Names were then taken and shares were subscribed to the value of £70. By the next meeting money had been raised to purchase both the ground and the huts. A committee was then formed with Mr Montgomery as President; W Valentine, Vice-President; Trustees W Adams, W Gentry, and W Ayres; C Bridges, Treasurer; W Young and W Grimwood, Committee. The ground was purchased and Messrs Baker, Hammond and Laver were engaged to dismantle and re-erect the huts on the newly-acquired site. The Committee arranged for supplies of drink from P Ellis of Shepherd Neame Ltd in the Cauliflower Inn. The Club was opened on 24th March, 1921, by A Goodes, who wished the Club every success. The Club was affiliated to the Club & Institute Union that September. Another building had to be added, but the premises were still too small and it was decided to apply to Shepherd Neame to borrow money to build a permanent Club. At the same time F Blows was offering the meadow adjoining the Club for sale at £800. An architect, Mr Wills, drew up plans for a new Club and estimates for that and the new meadow came to £5,000. A deputation of Messrs Montgomery, Adams, Bridge and Widows went to Shepherd Neame an, after long negotiations Mr Neame sanctioned loan of £5,000 at 5%.

The new Club opened on 15 September, 1925 and a new Concert Hall was added in 1929, built by W Cooper for £1,200, also borrowed from Shepherd Neame. That year G Hadingue was appointed Secretary. In 1931 a new Lounge was built by H Bradshaw for £700 but this was followed by a bad period, when takings fell to just £100 a week, giving merely £20 a week to cover all expenses. Work needed to be done on deteriorating pipes and Mr Neame again came to the rescue, had the pipes renewed and also reduced the loan interest to 4%. Things improved and in 1932 the roof of the Billiard Hall was jacked up and more bar space provided. The Shepherd Neame loan was finally extinguished by 1947.

Over the years the club has become renowned for its top quality entertainment. Prior to WW2, Vera Lynn was a frequent visiting artiste.

RWMC Silver Prize Band

RAINHAM SOCIAL CLUB

The Labour Club was built in 1925, in 1931 becoming the Social Club. Harry Hogg and Mr Samuels ran it jointly and paid off the mortgage to the brewers. After Mr Samuels retired, Mr Brennan took over and re-mortgaged the club to Courage Brewery for refurbishment. Sadly, while pebble-dashing the exterior, the memorial stone was covered.

Originally there were no windows on the right of the building, as it was near the Church Hall. When East Ham Council later bought it, they had windows installed.

By 1944 Taylor Walker's were supplying the club. Beer was fourpence a pint and sixpence would buy half a pint, 5 Woodbine cigarettes and a box of matches!

There was a bad incendiary bomb raid on 21st January, 1944, when a bomb went through the billiard table and Mr Samuels was injured. Mr Cook's 16 year old son was killed outside when he picked up an incendiary and put it in his pocket, where it exploded.

Beside the club was an entrance to a concert hall where the children went for the 'tuppenny rush' to see silent films. This is now part of the club, used as a billiard hall.

In the 1920s Haigh Hall was built next door with money provided by Earl Haigh to put up small memorial halls across the country. It was used for various functions, as well as being the first library. It was pulled down in the 1960s and St Helen's Court was built.

RAINHAM LITERARY SOCIETY

The Society was founded in 1879 as a Workmen's Institute and Reading Room, which continued until 1933 when it was absorbed by Essex County Libraries.

In 1967 the County Library moved from Upminster Road South to the current site in Broadway.

Rainham Football Team with Mrs. Ayres, 1927

RAINHAM OLD BOYS

The origin of Rainham Athletic Football Club stems from the days of Rainham Youth Centre – 1945/6/7 seasons. After two years in the services this minor side formed Rainham Old Boys, under the guidance of Charlie Cranfield, P A Wright and Mr Daniels (a Rainham school teacher). Norman Terrell was team captain who also played for Hornchurch and District, and Essex County.

Rainham Old Boys was considered by many as one of the strongest junior sides in the fifties. In 1953/4 the Essex Junior Cup was brought home to Rainham, which was no mean achievement, there being 365 clubs entering this competition. The season of 1957/8 gave the first and second teams the Thurrock and Thameside League and Cups - a 'double' double - an impressive performance.

Given below are the honours achieved:-

Winners Thameside League Cup		1948/9
Runners-up Thurrock League Comb. Cup		1951/2
do-		1952/3
Finalists Essex Junior Cup		1952/3
Winners	-do-	1953/4
Winners	Thameside League & Cup	1953/4
	Premier Div. A Section	- 1957/8
	First Div. B Section	- 1957/8

For a short time the name was altered to Rainham Social F.C., but in 1966 it was changed to Rainham Athletic Football Club.

Rainham Old Boys and their trophies

Rainham was the first known centre of coursing in Essex. The first recorded meeting was held in 1845, and continued intermittently until the marshes were sold to the War Office in 1906.

The Essex Union Hunt met at Rainham until the 1950s. Berwick Ponds at Abbey Woods, still provides good coarse fishing.

RAINHAM SCHOOL OF DANCING

Miss Eileen Woodhouse taught dancing in Rainham for 23 years. Her parents had purchased a plot of land in Parsonage Road after being bombed out of Plaistow, the building work was completed by 1951.

In 1954 Miss Woodhouse (centre of picture: Marion Jacobs, far right) started her dancing school in the little hut in Rainham Recreation Ground. Proceeds from the first show went to the P.D.S.A. who had a veterinary surgery in a van in the park twice weekly.

After demolition of the hut, the dancing school moved to the hall at the rear of the Cauliflower, but was soon usurped by the new bingo craze. Miss Woodhouse then approached the Minister of the Methodist Church who welcomed her intentions to provide the children with an alternative to playing in the strects. The school had 120 pupils with ages ranging from 3 years to adult.

Dawn Chandler, a former pupil of the Dancing School, reminisces:-

"Pupils were encouraged to take their examinations in tap and ballet. Two further branches opened, one in 'The Hut' at Wennington, and one at Aveley School. Nobody ever failed their exams with Miss Woodhouse. Some of her pupils went on to dance on cruise ships and travelled the world. One ex-pupil who later trained to be an opera singer went for an audition where there were two other applicants of equal aptitude, but she got the part because of the way she walked onto the stage - she was upright and poised like a dancer.

"I was 35 when I approached Miss Woodhouse, wanting to learn ballet as I had learned tap and acrobatics when I was a child. Miss Woodhouse asked me to get some mothers together for a class, but of course nobody of my age was interested. I was so fortunate when she let me join her class. I passed all my exams and later joined the Lightnin' Drama Group with Sue Sargent, where I taught girls to do the Charleston.

"Miss Woodhouse once put on a display in the Methodist Church where the small children danced to the Psalms, and received a standing ovation. She was like a mother to her pupils - gentle, kind, caring and very patient, she just loved her work and loved the children as if they were her own. They, of course, loved her too. She was an adjudicator, examiner and lecturer and went all over the country. She also updated syllabus for grades in tap, ballet, modern and acrobatics.

"After her retirement the Rainham branch was taken over by Miss Marion Jacobs, a very talented lady who now teaches floral art and has received many awards for her beautiful displays at the Chelsea Flower Show."

THE PLOTLANDERS

Many of the plotholders lived in hastily erected corrugated or wooden dwellings and then went on to build more substantial housing. They were liable for rates when they had curtains up and a yale lock on.

It wasn't until the late 1960s that many of the roads were adopted or tarmaced. Prior to this they consisted of mud and potholes, the owners constantly renewing the cinders outside their homes to form a footpath. Ernie remembers walking down Parsonage Road in the smog one bleak winter's evening, with his head down against the prevailing wind when, suddenly, he fell over a large object and landed in the road. After a closer look he discovered it was a donkey asleep on the roadway.

Mr and Mrs Cook with their son, Ernie, pictured outside the first bungalow they built on one third of an acre plot in Parsonage Road. The plot which has a 38ft. frontage and 400 ft. rear garden was purchased in 1923 for £50. A brick bungalow, also built by Mr Cook, later replaced the original building

As a teenager Ernie worked in Ferry Lane for Thompson Bayliss, who manufactured portable bungalows, sheds and chicken sheds. He went to Cranham with co-worker Howdy Byford (later to become a well known motorcycle ace), to erect a shed. It was another freezing day and as he got off the motorbike he fell into the road as his legs were completely numb, due to the cold weather.

PHYLLIS'S STORY

Phyllis, born at Southfields in 1921, remembers her Rainham childhood:-

"We moved to Rainham when I was 7 as my father, an architect and master builder, had purchased a plot in Parsonage Road where he built four bungalows. Plots were cheap and many Londoners moved here from the 1920s onwards.

My parents were very strict, I wasn't allowed to play in the street, so I would embroider or make dolls' clothes from offcuts of linen from my father's drawing board. The fabric softened and lost its blue colour when washed.

My mother had a cane on the back door and she wasn't afraid to use it. One day I tore my new dress when getting off the swing. She used it then allright!

Each Sunday in the fine weather we would walk through Berwick Pond Road to the White Hart in Hacton Lane, with Peter, our little West Highland Terrier, in tow. My parents would have their drinks and my brother and I would have a glass of lemonade and an arrowroot biscuit."

RAINHAM HORTICULTURAL SOCIETY.

Rainham Horticultural Society was formed in 1923 to cater for the plotholders, people mainly from the East End of London who built their homes on land purchased for £140 an acre or £20 a plot.

The Society offered plants and advice as well as arranging cheap weekend transport by lorries, with benches as passenger seats at a penny a ride, which met the trains at Rainham

Station. The RHS building opened in 1962 and is opposite Rainham Cemetery in Upminster Road North.

In 1963 the development of Brights and Parsonage farmlands was graphically described in the BBC Radio programme *Gardeners' Question Time* at the request of Miss M Waterman, secretary of the society.

Russell's Farm, also known as Bright's Farmhouse burnt down in the 1920s.
Soon after Brights Avenue was built on the site

THE CARAVANNERS OF LAKE AVENUE

The caravan site, owned by Mr Edward Bastow, was in the Thorn Lane/Stoke Road area of Lake Avenue. It was often in the news and brought notoriety to our quiet little backwater.

THE STORY OF A COURAGEOUS MOTHER

THE COURAGE OF A RAINHAM MOTHER, WHO SAVED THE LIFE OF HER SON ON 14TH MARCH, 1953.

Mrs Doris Botham, aged 28, of Lake Avenue went down a 6 feet deep shaft leading to an underground cesspool, held her boy up and clung to the edge of the cesspool for 25 minutes, until a neighbour arrived with ropes and a ladder.

The cesspool is on a caravan site owned by Mr Edward Bastow, where Mrs Botham lives with her husband and son. She was talking to her neighbour when she heard a splash. Running to the top of the cesspool, from which the canvas cover had been removed, she saw a pair of feet in the water. Though fully clothed she went down the hole and saw the boy's school cap floating on the surface. She grabbed the child and wedged herself in a corner of the cesspool, pulled him up and held him across her body until help arrived. Both mother and son made a full recovery from this terrible experience.

The caravan site was in the news again in February, 1957, *The Romford Recorder* pictured and reported:-

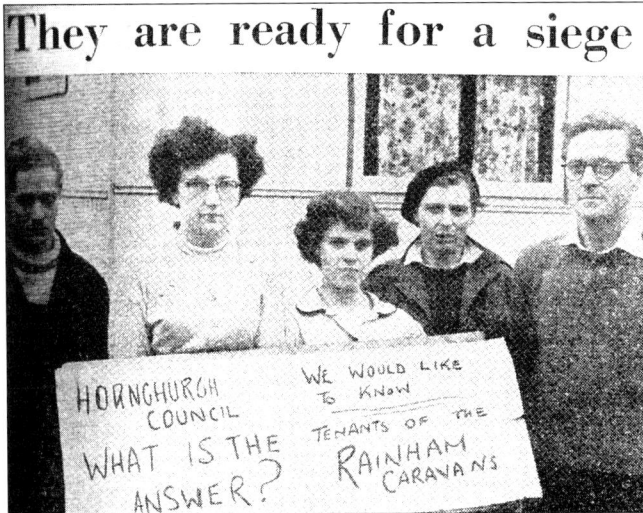

The caravanners of Lake Avenue, threatened with the loss of their homes under a High Court injunction, literally started digging in. A trench is being dug around the site and wheels have been taken off the caravans. The injunction perpetually restrains the site owner, Mr Edward Bastow, from keeping caravans on his land.

Their latest move confirms the intention declared by committee member, Mr Went, a month ago "We stay until they find us homes, or drag us out with tanks."

The colony is preparing for a state of siege.

Eight years later, on 29th January, 1965, *The Essex & Thurrock Gazette* reported:

The last two caravans were towed off the Lake Avenue site this week. Mr Bastow, his wife Joan and their three year old daughter remained in their caravan while council employees took down a section of corrugated iron fence from around the site, fixed Mr Bastow's caravan to the tractor and pulled it straight off. They parked it at the bottom of Lake Avenue.

Another of the caravans belonging to a family who had not been rehoused was taken off the site later the same day. Mr Reg Bennett a 38 year old window cleaner who had previously told *The Gazette,* "I'm not moving", had undone the wheelnuts on his caravan overnight and let down the tyres. He claimed Mr Bastow owed him at least £13 and he was not prepared to leave the site until he got the money. After more discussions his caravan was towed off. The site is scheduled for housing development.

LOCAL CELEBRITIES

THE REID TWINS

Marjorie and Constance Reid of Rothbury Avenue were invariably chosen to play the lead rôles in many of Rainham School's productions. Eve Sears had a far more important rôle - she sewed thousands of sequins on all the costumes. Professionally known as the Reid Twins, they were in fact the remaining two of triplets. They made several television appearances during the 1950s with their mirror act of acrobatic tumbling. They were were highly regarded and had many engagements at music halls throughout the country before appearing in *Television Music Hall* on 7th March, 1953. They were trained by their father.

The Reid Twins, with charity worker George Bentley of Romford
From the *Romford Recorder*

ED KING & THE RANCHBOYS

Left to right: Gerry Avery (lead guitar), Dennis Brown (steel guitar),
Hank Locklin (top U.S.A. Country and Western singer), Brian New (double bass),
Dawn King (female vocalist), Ed King (lead singer/rhythm guitarist), Ron White (fiddler).

Ed King, real name Albert Edward Watson, was born in Barking, 8th September, 1927. After his marriage to Dawn Chandler, in 1961, he lived in Brights Avenue, Rainham. He claimed to have been the man who introduced country music to Britain in the 1950s, and in his heyday, was voted Britain's top country singer for five consecutive years.

Dawn tells us a little of her life with her talented husband:-

"In 1946 Ed developed pleurisy and spent nine months bedridden, teaching himself to play the ukulele whist lying on his back. It was then that he wrote his first song 'World of Make Believe'. In 1948 he heard country music for the first time on *Hillbilly GuestHouse*, the singer being Hank Thompson. Ed didn't know what sort of music it was but knew he loved it and he bought his first guitar and taught himself to play. He played for friends, relatives, handicapped children (at Eastbury House), and the elderly, which gave him the confidence to turn professional and in 1952 he went on the road with Ed King and the Ranchboys.

"Ed and his brother, Dave, sang in harmony. Ed taught him how to play the ukulele, and they became known as the King Brothers, but another group were known by this name so they changed their name to The Mavericks. They played at many local venues, including Deri Park, Rainham, and were in Dagenham when Jack Fallon, an agent, came in, liked their style, and booked them They travelled to gigs on buses with all their equipment - they were together for s couple years. Ed went solo for a time, then met Gerry Avery, lead guitarist, at a party. He met Dennis Brown through his cousin. Dennis was playing Hawaiian music at the time, so they formed a trio. Gerry Dooley (agent) was in the audience and booked them for several gigs.

When Ed's band was on the radio in *A Cowboy Soap Opera* they were known as 'Sons of the Saddle'; when playing for Jerry Dooley they were 'Riders of the Range', same as the show. It all became very confusing. A Sergeant at USAF South Ruislip rang to book them to appear. They didn't have a name at that time, but when they arrived at the base there was a big poster outside announcing 'Ed King and the Ranchboys', the name had been chosen for them.

"I met Ed when he advertised for a singer. At the time I had a soprano voice, and had one month to learn to sing lower, and with an American accent. I learned two songs to sing solo, and two duets with Ed. I got the job, and was then known as Dawn King. I also played the auto harp and banjolele. I married Ed on my 20th birthday.

"We had many happy times, six of us, singing in harmony in the wagon for 200 miles or so, on the way to USAF bases and I was very proud to be part of that sound. Ed played for 14 years and estimated that he had travelled 1½ million miles playing one night stands. Ed had another band called 'The Country Boys' who played pubs and clubs all over England, and did recordings for BBC London Country and Radio Medway. He was with this band until he retired in 1972. Ed passed away in 1986 when he was only 58.

A few funny incidents come to mind: At a US Air Base one evening, Ed fired his gun and shouted 'Yer Hoo' and nothing happened, so in a meek voice said 'Bang'. The whole place erupted. At another venue they all let off a round and didn't realise there was a false ceiling, which was very low and made of polystyrene. They were all covered in white bits and it looked as if it was snowing. Ed was 6ft 4¼ and with 3" heel on his western boots he seemed a lot taller. "They played at Bentall's Restaurant one evening, having brought these great gnarled rubber feet with corns and hair coming out of the toes. The steel guitarist put one on a piece of wood and when he tapped his foot to the beat, the foot went up and down. The manager came over and asked them to remove it, as it was putting the diners off their meals!

"My daughters, Cindy and Anita, and I sing country songs in harmony. We have many recordings, the first when Anita was about 6, singing in harmony with her Dad, and Cindy and I singing 'Where Could I go but to The Lord', which is full of lovely harmonies. Cindy has written many songs, one called 'Daddy Wore a Stetson' dedicated to her Dad. They are both fine singers, their Dad would be so proud of them."

MR RAINHAM

Dr Deri Stephens, our local G.P. known to all as Mr Rainham

Dr Deri Stephens had supported many activities and contributed much to Rainham including Rainham Football Club, and their ground, Deri Park, was named in his honour. Dr Stephens of The Priory, Wennington, died in October, 1958 aged 58, leaving a wife Ruby and two children. Mrs Stephens had a children's fashion shop in Wennington Road called 'Penny Ray', next door to the practice her husband shared with Dr. Dunlea.

Shops in Wennington Road

Until the late 1950s Charlie Flint had a Dairy at the top of Cowper Road, near the junction of Wennington Road. His nickname was 'Shirty' Flint, as he always had the tail of his shirt hanging out. He sold milk from the premises and from a churn in his three-wheeled push cart.

He was very fit and an excellent runner, and would go in for races - which he invariably won - even when he was quite elderly.

Pieroth's had a Nursery in Wennington Road where Venette Close now stands. They grew tomatoes and cucumbers in greenhouses for the 'war effort', also dahlias. They also had another quarter acre further down the road.

ESSEX & THURROCK GAZETTE
During the 1960s the weekly newspaper dedicated a small section to a Rainham 'Personality'.
It is with their kind permission that we can, once again, enjoy the reminiscences of these lovely characters who are, sadly, no longer with us.

MRS MONTGOMERY IS RAINHAM BORN & BRED
Born in 1885 in a house in Rainham Broadway, Mrs Harriet Montgomery now has nineteen grandchildren and nine great grandchildren. Mrs Montgomery, who lives in Cowper Road, was one of five children born to a farm and factory labourer.
"When I was 11 I left the Upminster Road School," she told the *Gazette* this week. "The school - and the whole area - was very different then. There weren't all the houses in the roads round here then, just one or two." Mrs Montgomery started in domestic service after she had left school. For seven years she worked in houses at Brixton, Barking and Forest Gate. "When I was 18 I got married," she said. "That was young for those days. But I moved back to Rainham again and I've lived here ever since." Mrs Montgomery and her husband lived in Rainham Broadway before moving into the Cowper Road house 56 years ago.
Her husband was the First President of the Rainham Working Men's Club, and was for many years secretary. "When the Club was first open it was only a tin hut," she said. "The dances we held were the only thing to do in Rainham then. I was on the Ladies' Committee for many years. We used to run all the raffles and dances to raise money for the children's fund. I can remember sitting down about this time of year to make paper hats for the St Patrick's Day dance."

MR COOK'S FAMILY HAVE A 500 YEAR CONNECTION WITH RAINHAM
"My family goes back 500 years in the Parish Church records," says Mr Hart Cook of Ingrebourne Road, Rainham. A member of Rainham Working Men's club for more than 40 years, Mr Cook has been a local man all his life. He was born in Cowper Road, Rainham. "I was one of five children and went to school in the Upminster Road - Mr. Mace and 'Daddy' Hyatt taught there in those days. I left when I was 13 and started work on a local farm." When he was 15 he joined the Navy. "In those days you could join the Navy when you were younger," said Mr Cook. "In fact, I must have been one of the youngest people who served in the First World War." He was stationed in the Scapa Flow. "We had a special light cruiser and aircraft carrier," said Mr. Cook. "We carried just one aircraft on the front!"
A keen sportsman in his youth, Mr Cook had a full list of interests - he boxed, swam and played football for the navy, and in 1919 was 10 mile walking champion of Chatham Naval Barracks. "I did various jobs when I left the Navy in 1923," said Mr Cook. "With the mass unemployment you were glad to get any sort of work."
For the last 16 years Mr Cook has worked for a local bookmaker, he retires in 1964.

Mr Cook is proud of his family background. "There must be 500 people or more in this area linked in some way with my family," he said. "There are other names now, but they are all linked."

Mr Cook has two Police Recommendations, one for stopping a bank raid and another for holding up the roof of a house in Penerley Road while a child was dug out from the bombed ruins.

POSTMISTRESS FOR NEARLY 40 YEARS

For nearly 40 years Mrs Jane Holmes was Postmistress of Rainham. Now 80 years old Mrs Holmes, who lives in Wennington Road, left the Post Office service just after the last war.

She was born in Hollingbourne, Kent, one of 11 children. Leaving school at 13 she went straight into the Post Office. "I started as a telegraphist," she told the *Gazette* this week. "My father worked for the Post Office for some time, I was interested in the work and got the chance of a job."

When she was 17, Mrs Holmes left home and went to Minster on the Isle of Thanet. "I moved because I wanted to get on in life," she said. "I was a postal telegraphist at Minster for two years."

While she was there she saw an advertisement for a telegraphist in Rainham. She got the job and has been here ever since.

In the early years of this century, Rainham Post Office was not on its present site in Wennington Road. "In those days we were on the other side of the Church, where Paynes the butcher is now (at present the Goldmine) and then in 1907 we moved into the Broadway where the estate agents is (now Sackvilles)."

From 1907 until 1945 Mrs Holmes was Rainham postmistress. In the same year she took up this post she was married to a local man, son of an old Rainham family.

"We were terribly busy at the Post Office during the First World War," said Mrs Holmes. "We had to take all the calls for the musketry camp on the marshes and everything for Hornchurch Airfield. Every Sunday morning the war news would come through; I had to write it all down and put it in the Post Office window so that people could come and read it if they wanted to. There wasn't the newspaper coverage then."

When Mrs Holmes was young Rainham was 'a proper little village, it's very different now; in those days you knew everyone.'

MR SWANN KEEPS BUSY WITH TWO ALLOTMENTS

Born in Wennington in 1871, Mr. John Swann of Cowper Road, Rainham still, despite his age, keeps two allotments.

"My father worked at Rainham Creek," he said this week. "I can remember when I used to take tea down there for them; it must have been in the 1890s." When he was 7 he and his parents moved from Wennington to Rainham, and until he was 10 years old he went to school in Upminster Road. "I started work at Wennington, it was general farm work, really. Weeding onions. I remember particularly. We had a very wicked old man looking after us then. He dragged his wife all the way from Wennington down to the Creek once, and he used to come down and make sure we were working properly. If he didn't think we were, he'd cut us across the backside with his staff." But Mr. Swann didn't remain a farm worker for long!

His father bought him a set of tools and he became a carpenter, a trade he stayed in until he retired. First as an ordinary carpenter and later as a master and foreman carpenter. He worked all over Rainham, Hornchurch and Thurrock. He had a long connection with Thames Board Mills. He first went there in 1915, left when the whole factory went on strike, and returned in 1922, staying there until his retirement in 1946.

For more than 40 yrs. Mr Swann was a member of the Rainham Town Band and from time to time he helped out other bands - Aveley and Thurrock among them.

"But we never had the support after the Second World War that the football club had," he said, "and we wound up in 1961. I remember when the Rainham Working Men's Band won a shield at Alexandra Palace. I played for them as well."

MR DUNK LEFT SCHOOL AT 12

"When I was young there were only four streets in Rainham really," said Alf Dunk, of Evansdale, Dovers Estate. "All the rest was fields and allotments." Born in 1904 in Bridge Road, Rainham, Mr. Dunk has been in this area for a good deal of his life.

"I went to the School in Upminster Road, but in those days everything was different. Where the Upminster Road School is now was just allotments in those days."

Rainham Junior School, 1910

Mr. Dunk said that Bridge Road was very different then too. "We always had to live upstairs in the winter, because of the flooding," he said.

In 1916 when his father was in Kitchener's army, Mr Dunk moved with his mother to Barking. "I was only 12 when I left school, my dad was in the forces and I didn't like the school they sent me to at Barking. It was such a change going from a country school to a town school. I had to go before the Education Committee, and they asked me I wanted to stay at school or go out to work. I said I'd prefer work, and have been working ever since."

After 12 months at a glass works in Barking, Mr. Dunk took many jobs. Married in 1925, he moved back to Rainham and has lived here ever since.

During the war he was on government work clearing and making runways at airfields all over the country. "In 1944 I went to a coal site in Derby on bulldozer work, but a year later I was back in Rainham at the Phoenix Timber Company, and I've been here ever since."

One of Mr Dunk's hobbies is collecting money for the blind. He has been a member of Rainham Social Club since 1958, has been on the Club Committee for several years, and has been Vice-president for four years.

"Things have changed such a lot," he said. "When we were young we made all our own amusements, we had a very good football team at school, which we arranged on our own. I preferred Rainham as it was before," he went on, "it's nothing but a suburb of Hornchurch now. But in some ways the 'good old days' weren't as good as all that you know. The unemployment between the wars wasn't much fun: I was unemployed for five months at one time."

Brights Farm, around 1900

CHAPTER TWELVE

MYTHS & LEGENDS

No country village would be complete without its folklore. Rainham is no exception.

Some local dwellings are reputed to be haunted. In one house tapping sounds and footsteps frightened the girls in uniform who stayed there during the last war. A later resident said that she had got used to the mysterious sounds.

The Family Centre is also reputed to have a resident ghost. Two ladies who cleaned the offices there around 15 years ago often felt a 'presence' in the room with them. On several occasions they would smell bacon cooking and, at other times, the taps would be turned fully on when no-one had been in the vicinity. They nicknamed this 'spirit' Ada, and were convinced that it was the ghost of a resident of the old dwellings which had previously occupied this site. I would add that I know both ladies very well and they are not the type given to fancy!

A weird looking phantom who would glide along a bank between Frog Island and Fords was often seen by workers in the area. It was thought to be one of the victims of the plague of London - it was rumoured that the bones of many of these poor souls were buried in the mound in Manor Way. During the 1980s treasure hunters with their metal detectors would visit the mound where many clay pipes and ancient bottles were unearthed. Many of the Ford and Silcock & Colling workers were dubious about visiting the Frog Island site. One night a driver was having forty winks in his lorry when a ghostly head appeared at the top of the windscreen. It wasn't the phantom - just one of his workmates having a laugh!

Crossroads usually invite strange legends as they were often burial places of suicides and unfortunates. The junction of Lambs Lane and Wennington Road was known as The Wantz - an ancient name for crossroads. A few people claim to have heard a hollow sounding moan in this area.

There was a haunted house at Bluehouse Corner (the bend in Rainham Road near Victory Road). In 1913 my mother, then aged 5, was taken by her mother to a 'wise woman' known as Granny Farrance who lived in a cottage by Bluehouses, in order to have her warts charmed. The old woman apparently performed another service apart from witchcraft.

The junction of Gerpins and Warwick Lanes was once called Burnt Corner, and is shown as such on an 1839 tithes map. On the left is Gerpins Farm in the 1900s. Some people say it was so named from a barn which burnt down in the past. Others hold the tradition that a witch had been burnt at these crossroads. Witchcraft was prevalent in Essex in the past and in the 13th century the Archbishop of Canterbury ordered that all Church fonts be covered and locked to prevent the theft of consecrated water for purposes of sorcery. Rainham Church's ancient font still shows the marks made by this lock.

Like most God-fearing country women, my Gran was very superstitious and would eagerly read the annual *Old Moore's Almanac*, which she bought at the door each December.

My sister and I would sit, mouth agape, as Gran read, "Mother Shipton says we'll be knee deep in blood on London Bridge in the days to come." Why a prophetess - and a long dead one at that - who lived in a cave in Yorkshire, should worry about London beggared belief. Mind you, when I started work in 1962 at Adelaide House, London Bridge, I did tread a bit carefully.

17th century The Willows in Wennington , around 1910

Brick Farm, around 1900

CHAPTER THIRTEEN

CHANDLER'S CORNER

The area where Upminster Road, North & South, meets the A 13 (now A1306), is known as Chandler's Corner. Amelia and Albert Chandler, a baker by trade, moved to Rainham in the early 1900's when their young son, Frank, developed tuberculosis. It was thought that his health would improve by moving to the country.

Albert, who had worked for a baker in Edmonton, bought a piece of land in Rainham, and on Sundays would drive his family there for the day. People would come to Rainham countryside at weekends for a day out so Albert and Amelia started doing teas for the day trippers in her partly built villa. As it became more popular they introduced Sunday dinners. Amelia would peel the potatoes in the car on the way to Rainham to save time.

Albert and his two sons, Albert jnr and Frank built the chalet house, which they named Millbert Villa, next to the Grangewood Café. At that time the A13 went from Dover's Corner, through Rainham Village, along Wennington Road to the Lennard Arms.

In later years the road was re-routed through the centre of their vast plot where they kept many chickens amongst the fruit trees in their orchard (Orchard Avenue being built on the perimeter of this site).

Frank and his brother, Bert, would play football on their usual spot - which was, by this time, the A13 - they weren't disturbed too often by the traffic, as there were hardly any vehicles on this stretch of road in those days!

The baker's shop

WALL'S GARAGE

Alfred George Wall, founder of Wall's Garage, was lodging with his wife in Cowper Road when his first daughter, Alice, was born in 1895. He moved to no. 103, Wennington Road and opened up a cycle repair business, where he also made bikes. He was the proud owner of a pennyfarthing bicycle, which he hired out for 2/6d. (12½p) per day.

There weren't many bikes on the road in those days, so repairs were mainly confined to weekends. Alf decided to find other work to supplement his income, and gained employment as a stoker in a factory (possibly Salamon's) in Ferry Lane.

When the motor car became poular, he did repairs in the garage at the rear of his bike shop in Wennington Road. The business expanded and larger premises were required so he moved to the current site on the A13 near Chandlers Corner.

His grandson, Ray, tells us of Mr. Wall's eventful life:

"When Rainham Town Football Club played their first match on their new ground at Deri Park in 1948, they were playing with a new ball presented to them by their oldest supporter, Alf Wall, who was then 81 years old.

"He attended the old Rainham Village School in Upminster Road. It had only been erected two years when he became a pupil. He spent most of the time paying truant, getting the stick and jumping out of the window. He left at the age of 12 and started work picking potatoes on local farms at a wage of 3/6d per week.

"He left farm work at the age of 17 and for eleven years worked in the boiler room at a local factory, for 17 shillings a week. Cycling was coming into its own and while working at the factory Alf started a cycle shop as a sideline. In the shop, now occupied by The Wool Shop, Alf built his cycles; all types, the pennyfarthing being the most popular, with wooden frames, wooden wheels and steel tyres.

"He was married at Upminster Baptist Chapel at the age of 21. He lived at Rainham and the bride at Corbets Tey - there was nothing for it but to walk. They didn't have any donkeys or motor cars in those days, so Alf had to set off early morning and walk across to Corbets Tey (it was known as Cobbets Tye to Rainham people then) to pick up the bride. They took the best man with them and walked to Upminster. After the wedding they walked back to Rainham.

"He couldn't make the cycle shop a full time job as there weren't many cycles in Rainham then, but he started Rainham Cycle Club - now extinct - and the group of enthusiastic 'pioneers' of cycling wearing their colours - grey suits and light blue caps - became widely known in this part of Essex.

"Alf looked around for a new job, and it was about this time that Rainham Parish Council thought of lighting the streets. Fifty oil lamps were used and he became the first and last of Rainham's lamplighters. Every evening before dark he carried his ladder about the streets and in just under two hours had all the lamps from the green (where the War Memorial now stands) to the far end of Wennington Road, near The Lennard Arms, alight.

"In 1896 Alf, with a group of young men, started Rainham's football team. As village handyman he made the goalposts and erected them every Saturday, and marked out the pitch on the meadow where Rainham Police station now stands.

"In 1913 he found himself a job as caretaker at Rainham Cemetery and had only been working there for six weeks when the first grave he dug was for his wife. He was left a widower with 11 children.

Mr Wall's workshop in 1905
[Vestry House Museum, London Borough of Waltham Forest]

74

"He claimed to be the first man to sell petrol in Rainham. He cycled to Canning Town on his red white and blue penny farthing - which he helped to make just after the Boer War - and brought back half a gallon of petrol, which took him six weeks to sell.

"From this disappointing start he increased his sales of petrol when motor cycles came on the road. He took an interest in motorbikes and soon found that his shop in Wennington Road was not large enough.

"He erected the garage at Chandler's Corner in 1928."

EPILOGUE

Many changes have occurred in Rainham in recent years. The old butchers shop, Charlotte's Alley, and the terrace were demolished to make way for the Stanton Radio Building, now the Library, and the Family Centre. Small factory groups sprang up all over Rainham.

These happy workers were snapped at The Veneer, Lambs Lane, late 1950s.

Barclay's Bank and St. Helen's Hall were built. The Hollies, by this time derelict, made way for one of the two new parades of shops in Upminster Road South.

Thankfully, the Village centre still retains its historical core and community spirit, as this snapshot taken as a recent Christmas Fair, shows -

Our community has expanded, the shops have changed hands many times. Cramphorns, Hills, Flints and the Dairy are just a vague memory.

Hopefully with funds available for uplifting the Thames corridor and its surrounding area, Rainham could once again become the country village we knew and loved.

Rainham School pupils in 1937

ACKNOWLEDGEMENTS

I would like to thank the following for their help and encouragement, but, most of all, for their time

Ivy Allen, Evalda Attwood, Joan Axten, Irene Bailey, Charles Bifield, Tom Binding, Phyllis Blighton, Shirley Cannon, Bert Collis, Ernie Cook, Grace & Ellen Dalton, Ruth Daws, Jean Elsdon, George English, Branwell Evans, Sir Len Farram, Arthur Jacobs, Dawn Keeble, Fr Luke Kryanowski, Michael Melay, Mr Milne, Betty & Derek Pier, Pat Sanders, Dal Strutt, Paul Randell, Norman Terrell, Alf Viccary, Bert Walker, Ann Waller, Violet Watts, Eve Went, Eileen Woodhouse.

And a special 'thank you' to Jean Bond

for the many happy hours we have spent talking about the 'olden days'.

BIBLIOGRAPHY

Victoria County History of Essex

A History of Rainham – Frank Lewis

Essex & Thurrock Gazette

Romford Recorder